# Till the
# Boys
# Come Home

# Till the Boys Come Home

## HOW
## BRITISH
## THEATRE
## FOUGHT THE
## GREAT WAR

### ROGER FOSS

The
History
Press

## ALSO BY ROGER FOSS:

*May the Farce Be With You* (Oberon Books)

*Harden's Theatregoers' Handbook* (with Mark Shenton) (Hardens)

First published 2018

The History Press
The Mill, Brimscombe Port
Stroud, Gloucestershire, GL5 2QG
www.thehistorypress.co.uk

British Library Cataloguing in Publication Data.
A catalogue record for this book is available from the British Library.

ISBN 978 0 7509 6066 3

Typesetting and origination by The History Press
Printed and bound in Great Britain by TJ International Ltd.

# Contents

# Acknowledgements

This story wouldn't have been told without the generosity, advice and assistance of many people. Blanche Marvin MBE, a wise woman of immense depth of knowledge about theatre, encouraged me to develop the germ of an idea and then get it down on paper. As the project moved along, my friend of many years, the actor and comedian Peter John, shared his invaluable knowledge of music hall performers. Special gratitude goes to theatre critic and biographer Robert Tanitch for his constructive support and for allowing me to delve into his unique personal archive. Robert's book chronicling the London stage in the twentieth century is a compendium of information that no theatre researcher can do without. I am heavily indebted to The Stage Archive, to the ever-helpful archivists at the Central Library and John Rylands Library in Manchester and to the staff at Westminster Reference Library's performance art collection. Thanks also go to Rosy Runciman at the Cameron Mackintosh Archive, Mark Fox of the LW Theatres Group and to Becky Frankham at Stoll, an extraordinary institution providing homes and support for ex-servicemen and women that owes its origins to the remarkable charitable efforts made by many theatre professionals during the First World War. My ever-constant friend Liam Donnelly kept my feet grounded in the present whenever my head was immersed in the world of wartime theatre. Finally, some unknown people deserve extra-special gratitude: those long-forgotten journalists at *The Stage*, *The Era* and *The Performer* who reported the ups and downs of the national theatre scene on the Home Front. Without their column inches, some written up while Zeppelins were dropping bombs close to their Covent Garden offices, this story of theatre at war would have been just history, not human.

# Introduction

Why is it that everybody recognises 'Keep the Home Fires Burning'? What does 'Keep Right on to the End of the Road' have that other tunes from the First World War songbook don't? I remember thoughts like this going through my mind in 1963 when, in a previous life as a teenage actor, I appeared as a pierrot in a repertory company music hall show, which was probably riding on the back of the success of the pierrot-soldiers in *Oh, What a Lovely War!* Beatlemania was all the rage. And yet it seemed as if these old songs were just as powerful as 'She Loves You'. In performance the music and lyrics had a kind of semi-mystical communal power over the audience. Just like the Fab Four. It was extraordinary.

Fifty years later, I happened to be at Brick Lane Music Hall in East London watching a Remembrance Day show that was nearly all First World War melodies. The venue was full. Everyone joined in. This was extraordinary too: a new generation responding to songs composed almost a century ago as if they had entered the cultural DNA. Then it hit me. These were not just patriotic war songs, but songs skilfully designed to be shared communally – theatre songs: not recording studio songs. What was it like singing along to them when the lyrics were fresh and new, I wondered. What was it like hearing them for the first time inside a packed local Frank Matcham–designed Empire or Palace when war was intervening in every aspect of life? How did the shows they were written for and the performers manage to go on when Armageddon was being unleashed across the English Channel and everyone at home was living in a militarised total war economy?

I was curious. I looked for answers. I found some excellent comprehensive histories of Home Front society and culture. Most surveyed the wartime theatrical world in passing. Some ignored it altogether. Others emphasised theatre's morale-raising role. I discovered insightful scholarly research and unearthed powerful critiques of wartime theatre by critics who actually lived through the upheaval. When I read dusty memoirs of barely remembered actors and performers, my view of the period altered. It changed even more once I started poring over wartime editions of the theatre magazines of the time and read the weekly trade press. My assumptions about Edwardian theatre soon went out of the window. I didn't realise how vast the industry was when war broke out, how labour-intensive, and how ferociously commercialised everything was, with powerful syndicates dominating the variety and 'straight' sides of the business. Or how wide-ranging and exciting the stage could be for audiences entering a glamorous world of plays and twice-nightly variety. Even with cinema's rising popularity, theatre still dominated cultural life.

It soon became clear that the industry and the people working in it, onstage and off, faced unprecedented challenges and played a far more diverse and direct part in the war than I had imagined.

During four years of tremendous wartime activity, a curious yet absolutely fascinating hybrid of high drama, hilarious comedy and hideous tragedy emerged where star actors, low-rung performers, backstage staff and managements alike faced the same daily challenges of life as everyone else, such as conscription, fuel restrictions, food rationing and travel disruption, as well as Zeppelin and Gotha raids. Even when more and more stage professionals were going off to fight in real theatres of war, somehow British theatre had to keep right on to the end of the road. The task I set myself was to see how it eventually got there: to try and tap into the vibrant energy and the darker moments, partly through the fascinating minutiae of theatrical life written down on the spot by reporters and critics working for journals such as *The Stage*, *The Era* and *The Play Pictorial* while setting this 'hidden history' within the grander scheme of things. Having entered this world, it didn't feel dated or 'lost'; and although the mindset of the time is miles apart from ours, I couldn't help but admire these actors, entertainers, writers, musicians, backstage staff and impresarios at war. Many of them ended up buried in the graves of France. Others survived to become part of an emerging new theatre and popular entertainment environment. More than a century later, the legacy of changes in the composition of audiences and the way theatre is financed is with us still, a legacy that it is easy to forget was partly bred by war.

In many respects, five years before August 1914, British theatre was already poised for military action. That's why I had to begin this book in the West End of 1909. Spy dramas and invasion scare plays were pulling in audiences at a time when armaments were building up, the Anglo–German naval race was hotting up and Britain's home defence capability had become a political hot potato. One headline-hitting play, *An Englishman's Home*, tapped in to the anxieties of the moment and, for a brief period, was transformed from a first-night sensation into an augury for the future role of wartime theatre – a practice run for things to come.

# Prologue

༄༅༅

# 1909

'This is not a play: it is a national drama – an inspiration in patriotism'

It is 27 January 1909. A foggy day in London town. The British Museum has lost its charm: so have most of the city's familiar landmarks on this chilly Wednesday. For three days a dense yellow fog has ground the capital city to a halt. As night falls, a news reporter ventures beyond Fleet Street to discover London 'as dark as a bag ... a nightmare city with deserted, noiseless streets'.[1] At least a glimmer of gaslight emanates from the West End playhouses and music halls where the star turns of variety and the great actor–managers and glamorous actresses of the Edwardian stage reign supreme.

In 1909, London was the play-producing centre of the British Empire. The city had more theatres than ever before (fifty-four playhouses and fifty music halls) and the building boom was about to reach a new peak, with the opening of the London Palladium only two years away. But on a pea-souper night like this, theatreland's big hitters couldn't draw the crowds. The cast of *The Merry Widow*, in its third year at Daly's in Leicester Square, faced a half-empty house. It was the same glum picture at the

Comedy, where Marie Tempest was starring in Somerset Maugham's divorce drama *Penelope*. At the New Theatre in St Martin's Lane, matinee idol Lewis Waller (his female fans wore buttons inscribed 'KOW' – Keen On Waller) gave his patriotic Henry V to a few brave admirers. Even people's favourite Marie Lloyd at the recently refurbished Tivoli in the Strand, and sexy male impersonator Vesta Tilley (billed as 'Britain's Best Boy') at the Palace, were playing to vacant seats. At the Duke of York's, just along from the New, the high-flying children in J.M. Barrie's *Peter Pan* were grounded. Almost opposite, thick fog sneaked into the auditorium of Oswald Stoll's luxurious new London Coliseum, making it impossible to see the stage. The first 'turn' on the variety bill that anyone could pick out was 'The Howard Brothers and their flying banjos'.[2]

Meanwhile, in Charing Cross Road, the yellow murk swirling around Wyndham's Theatre filtered backstage where, just before 8.30 p.m., actors waited nervously in the wings for the curtain to rise on the premiere of an unknown play by an unknown author credited in the programme only as 'A Patriot'. *An Englishman's Home*, the first play to be presented at Wyndham's by actor–manager Gerald du Maurier (in 1904 he created the role of Captain Hook in *Peter Pan*), was the only production in the West End where real fog oozing from the street became indistinguishable from fake fog wafted by stagehands across the set. By strange coincidence, the play's opening scene took place in the living room of a middle class villa on the Essex coast cut off from the outside world – by three days of fog. But if there was a meteorological confluence at Wyndham's on that January evening, it wasn't just the foggy brew. Opening night sparked the first act in a five-month public drama that transformed an elegant Louis XVI-style London playhouse into a semi-militarised zone and a platform for war propaganda.

On the surface, *An Englishman's Home* begins as a domestic comedy centred around the middlebrow Brown family taking things easy on Boxing Day. But after a band of Teutonic-looking soldiers ('Nearlanders') had invaded their cozy world, then killed two Browns bravely defending hearth and home, the play went beyond the footlights and found itself at the epicentre of an explosive national narrative about homeland defence and preparedness for war. The story of this outwardly unassuming West End play's social and political impact not only demonstrates how deeply Edwardian popular theatre could influence national agendas; it rapidly developed into a dress rehearsal for the main drama, when the entire British theatre industry went to war.[3]

'The stirring drama aroused a fervid martial enthusiasm in the audience,' reported the *Daily Mirror* after a first night judged by the press as heralding an instant smash hit. According to the *Daily Express*, in the foyer afterwards men and women 'could be heard excitedly discussing the play, so wrapped up in it that many of them had no thought of supper, cabs, or home'. But, although obviously enthralling, it took an American critic to sense that the play had transformed Wyndham's stage into a wider public arena overnight: 'It is a national drama – an inspiration in patriotism.'[4] At a precisely the moment when British home defence policy was undergoing a politically controversial transformation in the years leading up to 1914, 'A Patriot' had pitched an English Everyman's

*An Englishman's Home*: Mr Brown discovers his son shot through the heart by the Nearlanders. (*The Play Pictorial*/Author)

front room into the front line of an imaginary invasion scenario, employing powerful images of disrupted domesticity that dredged up all sorts of underlying fears and fantasies about the nation under threat from German military might. For *The Times* reviewer, this was as topical as you could get:

> *An Englishman's Home* furnishes startling testimony to the hold which the great National Defence question has taken of the thoughts and imagination of the English public … for here is a play all about our national shortcomings, our lack of military defence, and, still more, our habit of pooh-poohing any endeavours towards reform. This play is absolutely made up of public questions.[5]

The *Observer* critic concurred, welcoming 'a play with a purpose' that 'illustrates reconsistently the attitude of those who either in spirit or in deed are willing to leave our unsystematic system of territorial defence to look after itself.'[6]

Next day, at Wyndham's, you were lucky to get in. With the mass circulation press grandstanding the production – 'This tract for the times should be seen by all who have the love of their country at its heart,' urged the *Daily Express* – who wouldn't want to queue up to see what all the fuss was about. As the production entered its second week, Herbert Jay, the theatre manager, had never known anything like it, selling more than £200 worth of tickets in one day. 'Long queues of people have been standing outside the box office, almost struggling, you might say, to obtain seats,' he told the *Express*: 'People are booking as far ahead as the end of March. We could easily fill several theatres nightly.' On top of that, Jay was inundated with applications from patriotically minded actors and actresses eager to join the cast of planned touring companies.[7]

Of course, the play caught on because it not only stoked up national nervousness about Britain's military capability; it also fleshed out the drama with recognisable contemporary 'types' speaking in everyday lingo, as familiar to theatre audiences then as television sitcom characters are to us today. But however 'in the moment' the play may have appeared to play-goers and critics alike, a *New York Times* reviewer offered a blunt reminder that it was just another moment in British theatre's notorious long-standing history of raising flag-waving martial enthusiasm.

> Nothing seems likely to restore the usual English calm and self-complaisance until the Army has been put on a genuine war footing and the Navy prepared to meet the combined fleets of Europe. What Charles Dibdin's sea songs did for the Navy one hundred years ago, *An Englishman's Home* is fast doing for the Army.[8]

In 1909 Germanophobia underpinned this particular invasion scare plot. In the 1790s, Francophobia informed populist patriotic theatre. In Victorian theatre there was an established tradition of patriotic displays and colonial melodramas, especially during the Crimean War. From John of Gaunt's speech in praise of England as 'this sceptered isle' in *Richard II* to images of a divided nation in *King John*, Shakespeare's assumed patriotic voices were often appropriated for banner-waving purposes, not least in 1914 when Henry V's Agincourt speech, as delivered by the great Edwardian thespians, took on a thrilling new sense of nationalistic urgency. During the pre-1914 years it was quite normal for London and provincial productions to whip up militarism: short plays and sketches with titles such as *Wake up England*, *Nation in Arms* and *A Plea for the Navy* regularly appeared. British music hall was, after all, where the term 'Jingoisim' was coined during the Franco–Prussian war when G.H. Macdermott ('The Great Macdermott') sang:

> We don't want to fight, yet by Jingo! if we do,
> We've got the ships, we've got the men, and got the money too.

Indeed, as a spreader of patriotic zeal, the historian J.A. Hobson regarded music hall as more potent than church, school, political meetings and the press:

As the only truly 'popular' art form of the present day, its words and melodies pass by quick magic from the Empire or the Alhambra over the length and breadth of the land, re-echoed in a thousand provincial halls, clubs, and drinking saloons, until the remotest village is familiar with air and sentiment. By such process of artistic suggestion the fervour of Jingoism has been widely fed.[9]

Hobson had a point. By 1909, even with cinema gaining in popularity, theatre-going was an incredibly strong cultural thread in the social fabric of pre-war Britain, with the old vulgarities of music hall beginning to give way to the more socially inclusive respectability of variety – so respectable that the Palace Theatre played host to the first Royal Variety Performance in 1912. A widespread network of lavishly appointed provincial theatres, many of them smelling of newness, was not only a powerful economic driver in the Edwardian entertainment industry but the conduit of choice for conveying nationalistic enthusiasm to a mass audience. By all accounts, however, no 'By Jingo!' cheers greeted the end of Act One of *An Englishman's Home*; just pin-drop silence when the mood changed from the jolliness of the Brown family gathering to the horror of a helmeted horde of Nearlanders bursting through the fog to execute Mr Brown on his own smartly trimmed lawn, while a poorly trained Territorial squad dithered about like an Edwardian Dad's Army. The shock of seeing this living nightmare onstage was clearly genuinely felt. As *The Times* noted: 'The grotesque, rather squalid, farce of the thing is turned to grim horror.'[10] Suddenly in 1909, popular theatre, defenders of the realm, recruiters of men, believers in the nobility of patriotic self-sacrifice, the press and a large section of the military establishment were all briefly marching together, though nobody could have known that this was a test run for what would happen in theatres between 1914 and 1918 on an industrial scale.

Politically, the play's 'be prepared' warning was as clear as daylight – playing at soldiers in the newly established voluntary Territorial Force of part-timers, which had been steered through Parliament by Lord

7458 E   ROTARY PHOTO. E.C.                    "AN  ENGLISHMAN'S  HOME."
          MR  CHARLES  ROCK                      MR  EDMUND  MAURICE              MISS  ELAINE  INESCORT
            AS  "MR.  BROWN."                      AS  "PRINCE  YOLAND."            AS  "MAGGIE  BROWN."
          PRINCE  YOLAND:  "YOU  ARE  A  CIVILIAN;  YOU  HAVE  BEEN  FIGHTING;  YOU  MUST  PAY  THE  PENALTY."

Grim moment: a postcard depicting the tense scene where Mr Brown is about to be taken out and shot. (Author)

Haldane, Minister of War, and officially came into law in April 1908, was not adequate enough to repel a highly trained invading army intent on marauding across the fields of coastal Essex. The Browns (and by implication all true Brits) were living in a vulnerable fool's paradise. For Haldane and the military top brass eager to enlist even more civilian volunteers for a Citizen's Army, here was a propaganda gift handed down from showbiz heaven. But *An Englishman's Home* immediately became sure-fire ammunition for highly vociferous Empire loyalists and old 'Soldiers of the Queen' from the National Service League, most of them still brooding over the Boer War, who had been lobbying for years for an Army based on compulsory national military service. Haldane must have only half-smiled when he read a *Daily Express* editorial semaphoring salient points to its readers:

Viscount Esher and Field Marshall Lord Roberts share the cover of a theatre magazine with leading actor Charles Rock. (*The Play Pictorial*)

Haldane might do worse than arrange with the manager for free performances of *An Englishman's Home* in every town in the country. It should be an admirable recruiting agent for his citizen Army. We trust, however, that the country will realise that voluntaryism is a hopeless system. The only way to arrive at a powerful and sufficient Army for home defence is for every young man to be compelled to undergo a period of military training. The possible good that may follow the production of *An Englishman's Home* can hardly be exaggerated. Every patriot will desire its success.[11]

Haldane took his seat at Wyndham's within days of the opening night, alongside a corps of high-level government ministers. At least two visits were made by Field Marshal Lord Roberts, president of the National Service League, which had been calling for the introduction of peacetime conscription, and by Viscount Esher, Chairman of the Territorial Association of the County of London, who jotted in his diary: 'A play of "invasion" most excitingly acted.'[12] These two stern-looking warriors found themselves featured as unlikely cover boys for the February issue of *Play Pictorial*, above an image of leading actor Charles Rock as Mr Brown.[13] But General Douglas Haig, who was serving in the War Office General Staff implementing the defence reforms, sat rather more thoughtfully alongside his wife, Dorothy. In his diary for 3 February, Haig wrote:

It is extraordinary how the play draws houses every night and how impressed the audience seem to be with the gravity of the scenes. I trust that good may result and that 'universal training' may become the law of the land, but for myself, the performance was not an interesting sight. I felt that the incapacity of the whole of the people in defending their homes was disgusting.[14]

By then, Haig, like anyone else in Britain who read a newspaper, would have known that the true identity of 'A Patriot' was Gerald du Maurier's

Cartoon illustration on the cover of the programme for *An Englishman's Home*. (Author)

older brother, Major Guy du Maurier DSO of the Royal Fusiliers, on active service in South Africa. Guy, who attended Sandhurst at the same time as Haig, had never written a full-length play before, but sent the manuscript to his actor brother Gerald, who was about to take up a tenancy at Wyndham's. Gerald recognised the box office potential and, with some script doctoring by J.M. Barrie, went ahead and presented the play without his brother's knowledge. When news of the sell-out success reached Guy at his outpost of Empire he wired cablegrams home, including one to the *Daily Express* emphasising the play's propagandising intent: 'Thanks for your congratulations. Cannot say much. King's Regulations seal my lips. If there are any lessons in the play hope it will run till they are learnt.'[15] At the same time, in a letter to his family, he enclosed a copy of an essay entitled 'The Insecurity of our Home Defence Today' published in the August 1908 edition of the literary journal *The Nineteenth Century And After*, in which reference was made to the fate of untrained civilian reserve volunteers who attempted to oppose an invading force. 'This is what we must rub in,' Guy scribbled in the margin of an article shot through with anxiety about possible 'national ruination'.[16]

The author of this argument for a policy of compulsory national service was Lieutenant Colonel Sir Lonsdale Augustus Hale, military correspondent for *The Times*, who is credited with the first use of the phrase 'Fog of War'. Which takes us straight back to the Wyndham's, where the January fog had long disappeared and the theatre had turned into a proxy recruitment centre. Fast forward to the first year of the war and almost all playhouses, variety theatres and music halls in cities and towns across the British Isles are providing public recruitment platforms, with artists often making direct appeals from the stage and recruiting officers waiting in the wings ready to sign up eager volunteers. A canny *Daily Mirror* leader writer had a premonition of things to come on the wartime theatre front:

WHY NOT

# BE THE FIRST TO

# MEET THE INVADER

# IN ESSEX

which is the area allotted to the

# LONDON CYCLIST REGIMENT

═ For further particulars apply at ═

FULHAM HOUSE, PUTNEY BRIDGE, S.W.

or to one of the Members of the

Regiment in attendance outside this

═══ Theatre in uniform. ═══

## LOCAL HEADQUARTERS ALL OVER THE METROPOLIS.

*Above and opposite:* Recruitment leaflets distributed at Wyndham's Theatre during the run of *An Englishman's Home.* (Author)

# HOME DEFENCE!

## RECRUITS WANTED FOR THE LONDON TERRITORIAL FORCES.

¶ **YOU** will see to-day the necessity of learning how to defend your homes.

¶ **Do not hesitate or delay!**

¶ A Recruiting Station has been opened at Nos. 20-22, CECIL COURT, CHARING CROSS ROAD, 30 seconds from this Theatre, where you can be **attested at once** for any arm or branch of the Territorial Force.

¶ Office open 9 to 11 a.m., and 6 p.m. to 12 midnight, except on Matinee days when the office will be open from 9 a.m. till midnight.

Attestation Forms can be obtained at any time of the day on application at the above address.

# DEFENCE NOT DEFIANCE

The great days of the pulpit when men filled big churches or stood in the open streets to hear some new doctrine expounded with much banging of fists and thumping of Bibles appear to be over. The sermons that are most effective come in dramatic form from over the footlights … Let patriots and organisers, men of ideas and hopers for reform, take courage from the example of Wyndham's Theatre. Let them not be afraid, in future, of using the stage as pulpit. It is far more effective, in this way, than any number of speeches in Parliament or from the platform.[17]

Wyndham's had effectively become a second home for London Territorial regiments. Recruiting sergeants waited outside each evening to catch potential amateur warriors as soon as they left the exits. Captain R.N. Kelsey, a member of the National Defence Association, who had offices at 20 and 22 Cecil Court, just a few yards from Wyndham's box office, arranged to swear in Territorial recruits there after every performance. Another company in Cecil Court, Graham & Latham, manufacturers of rifle range equipment, also lent their premises for recruitment purposes. By 11 February, the *Daily Mirror* discovered Captain Kelsey doing a brisk trade and appealing for the assistance of experienced recruiting sergeants: 'A word of encouragement and explanation from them would induce many men, who at present pass on, to come inside and enlist.' When, on the back of the play, Lord Esher launched a major *Daily Mail* campaign to enlist 11,000 men to complete the establishment of the London county battalions, within a few days 2,000 men answered the call.[18] No sooner had George R.F. Shee, Secretary of the National Service League, seen the play than he made arrangements for copies of his 1901 pamphlet *The Briton's First Duty: the Case for Conscription* to be available in the foyer along with a new League manifesto pressing for compulsory military training. Shee took this step, he explained, because:

The play is the very best instrument that could have been created to attract, in the first instance, and then to convert an apathetic public to the great reform which the National Service League has been working for.[19]

Roger Pocock, founder of the paramilitary Legion of Frontiersmen in 1904 to be 'the eyes and ears of the Empire', even urged Wyndham's management to use programmes and ticket envelopes to publicise the Territorials. But another Boer War veteran got there first. Captain A.H. Trapman, Adjutant of the London Cyclist Battalion, was so impressed on the opening night that he immediately bought advertising space in the programme giving contact details of all Territorial units in the London District, plus a full-page flyer insert proclaiming:

WHY NOT BE THE FIRST TO MEET THE INVADER IN ESSEX[20]

Soon there was far more information about Territorials in the programme than about the cast. Even the cartoon illustration on the cover – a satirical swipe at 'the modern young man' more interested in following football than defending the nation – was designed by Private Ernest Ibbetson of the London Regiment (Artists).[21] For a few months, any 'modern young man' attending any London theatre hoping for an escapist night out was obliged to listen to patriotic messages megaphoned across the footlights. Territorial officers turned up during intervals to call men to enlist, in exactly the same way that they would when war became a reality. Local big-wigs trod the boards to preach the message too; the *Express* reported how several London mayors 'are delivering five-minute recruiting speeches from music hall and theatre platforms'. As well as evangelising mayors, London music hall audiences were faced with a Biograph screen during the interval announcing:

### TO THE YOUNG MEN OF LONDON
11,000 patriotic men wanted NOW for the London Territorial Force

Those willing to respond to the national appeal should address a postcard to 'Territorial', the Daily Mail, London, E.C.[21]

Not everyone approved of the idea of theatrical recruitment. A *Manchester Guardian* editorial attacked the 'degrading' sight of uniformed soldiers taking to the music hall stage:

> The appearance of a Colonel of Territorials with his officers on the stage of a music hall after a 'patriotic' song sung by a comedienne (we believe that is the proper term) and the subsequent appeal to men to join the colours is, it must be emphatically asserted, degrading to the King's service and to the nation at large.[22]

Degrading or not, the sight of officers onstage became all too familiar in wartime Britain; and Edwardian comediennes (and comedians) were especially adept at appealing to audiences. Long before 1909, Britain's variety houses had become a sort of live national broadcaster of topically themed comedy sketches, playlets and catchy pop songs, frequently composed, rehearsed and inserted in an act at the last minute. Just days after *An Englishman's Home* made headlines, a jaunty recruiting ditty ('Won't You Join the Territorials?') found a slot in *Dick Whittington* at the Theatre Royal Drury Lane. They were quick off the mark at the Coliseum too, where baritone, actor and silent film director Leo Stormont presented a new patriotic multimedia item using a series of moving pictures depicting *England Invaded (as it would be)* and *England Invaded (as it should be)*. According to *The Stage*, Stormont's performance aroused 'considerable enthusiasm' with a turn that was clearly influenced by the home defence scare raised in Guy du Maurier's invasion scenario. It was no surprise for anyone attending *Cinderella* during its final week at the Adelphi to see Australian musical comedy star Carrie Moore introduce a specially written number, 'Bravo, Territorials'. This rousing marching song was soon performed by music hall acts in theatres across the country, published in sheet music form and recordings made by several different singers, before being played at homes on parlour pianos and whistled in the streets by errand boys – more or less the same route taken by most

Trade press advertisement for a
new song with patriotic appeal.
(*The Stage*)

MISS ELLA

# SHIELDS'

Greatest London Song 'Hit,'

## BRAVO,

## TERRITORIALS!

(While Jack is busy on the Sea)

NOW RELEASED FOR PANTOMIME ONLY.

*PRINCIPAL BOYS, MANAGERS, ETC., APPLY
FOR FREE PANTO RIGHTS IMMEDIATELY OF*

THE

# LAWRENCE
# WRIGHT MUSIC CO.,

8, Denmark Street (Charing Cross Road),
LONDON, W.C. 'Phone: Regent 155.

popular songs during the war, when soldiers transported catchy hits from West End shows to the trenches.[23]

Meanwhile, offstage, the voluntary concept got a boost when the Alliance Assurance Company announced that clerks joining the company would be required to join the Territorial Force and attend drills and training camps. More than 200 firms in London and 300 in the provinces soon signed up to a similar scheme. The day after Leo Stormont first unleashed his bravado act on Coliseum audiences, the theatrical link was clearly in Lord Haldane's mind when he congratulated a gathering of employers, describing how the lead of employers, newspapers, and a play had 'stirred the public imagination' and spread like wildfire:

> Instead of the old volunteer and militia forces, the country now has a force which is based on the capacity for rapid mobilisation; a much more businesslike force than was the case in the old auxiliary forces.[24]

For a nation supposedly at peace, Britain seemed to be gripped by an epidemic of khaki fever spread by a West End play. Territorials paraded as never before. Saturdays became 'Territorial Day'. 'Thousands cheer Saturday's marches' trumpeted the *Daily Mirror* headline for a news item that paid tribute to *An Englishman's Home* as the catalyst for the Territorial revival.[25] Determined not to be out-marched by city clerks, theatre professionals were as keen to join in 1909 as they were when the call to arms came in 1914. Actor Charles C. Ommanney wrote to *The Stage* proposing the formation of 'a company of Territorial mounted infantry' consisting solely of members of the theatrical and variety professions. Producer Charles Manners of the Moody-Manners Opera Company urged fellow theatricals to join up after reading about *An Englishman's Home* whilst on tour:

> There must be thousands of professional men who could easily devote an afternoon to drill: indeed, with musical comedies, comic operas and plays running regularly throughout a long tour, and with few or no rehearsals,

I should think they would be rather glad to have something to do in the way of drill, target practice, etc.[26]

The press interest in *An Englishman's Home* did not stop with the reviews. It did not stop with the succession of earnest leader columns. Cast members were interviewed and became overnight celebrities. Production photographs were everywhere. In a new *Daily Mirror* section aimed at women readers, Mrs E. Nevill Jackson wrote about 'What Mothers May Learn' from the play:

> To every thinking woman who sees the profoundly interesting play at Wyndham's Theatre, these questions must present themselves sooner or later: What am I doing for my country? How am I training my children or influencing those around me to listen to the great call the Empire is making? Courage, devotion and a vital sense of fatherland should be deliberately cultivated in the minds of boys and girls.[27]

The headline-grabbing continued. In early March 1909 the first UK touring production hit the road, opening at the Shakespeare Theatre at Clapham Junction. By the end of April, four separate companies were touring simultaneously. *The Stage* described how the play 'makes a triumphant entry into the provinces … the enthusiasm of Birmingham play-goers may be taken as typical of the country in general'.[29] The original London production eventually ran its course, closing on 19 June, by which time hundreds of thousands of people had seen it and the Territorial Force numbered more than 268,000 officers and men. Recruitment had flourished as if war really was around the corner, even if the full target establishment of just over 312,000 men was never achieved. If this was a high-water mark of the Territorial Force, it was also the moment when theatre rose up and showed its patriotic potential. It was only a matter of a few years before duty called once more and theatres everywhere, and the entire entertainment industry, began to weather the storms of war on a scale that nobody could have foreseen.

But on a Saturday night in June 1909, as soon as the scenery, costumes and propaganda leaflets were packed up, Wyndham's reverted back to its civilian role as a rather elegant West End playhouse. As for playwright Lieutenant Colonel Guy du Maurier DSO, 3rd Battalion, Royal Fusiliers, on 9 March 1915 he was killed in action by a German shell while serving in the trenches east of Kemmel in Flanders. In the same week, the 'Actors and the War' column in *The Stage* announced that more than 800 theatre professionals who took the colours had died in the first seven months of war.[30]

Almost fifty years later, on 29 June 1963, the fog of war hovered over Wyndham's Theatre again when Joan Littlewood's production of *Oh, What a Lovely War!* transferred from the Theatre Royal Stratford. In the theatre where *An Englishman's Home* urged preparation for war, another hushed audience looked at the experience in the trenches of the Somme and Passchendaele, retold in a show anchored in the vibrant variety and concert party entertainment of Edwardian Britain. The programme notes described how the company devised the production using information gleaned from official records, war memoirs and personal recollections, including the papers of Field Marshal Earl Haig.[31] One can only imagine how Haig, sitting thoughtfully in the stalls at Wyndham's in 1909 watching Guy du Maurier's play, might have reacted had he known that more than half a century later, on the exact same stage, he would be depicted as a 'donkey' leading 'lions' to slaughter and no longer the architect of victory after four dramatic years when the fog of war filled every theatre in the land and shrouded the entire nation.

# 1

## 1914

### Theatres as usual?

London, Whitehall, Tuesday, 4 August 1914, 10 p.m.. Unless a miracle occurs before 11 p.m. when the British ultimatum runs out, war with Germany is inevitable. While crowds swarm around Trafalgar Square waiting for Big Ben to strike, Ramsay MacDonald, leader of the Labour Party, is at a meeting in Whitehall. Someone mentions that although war is inevitable it will be 'most unpopular'. 'Rubbish,' MacDonald snaps: 'It will be the most popular war this country ever engaged in. Look out of the windows now and you will see the people beginning to go mad.'[1] On the stroke of 11 p.m., the hurrahs and anthem singing grows madder than the madness of Mafeking night. Adding a surreal touch to the frenzy, taxicabs taking men and women in posh evening dress home to the suburbs after an evening at the theatre attempt to inch through the throng. Somewhere, in the middle of it all, a man of the theatre stands alone quietly, soaking up the atmosphere.

Comedian George Robey knew all about appearing in front of big gatherings, only now Britain's 'Prime Minister of Mirth' made himself invisible. No one noticed the comedian, who was headlining a variety

Idealised patriotism on stage: the final tableau in the revue *Not Likely* at the Alhambra, with actresses Miss M. Thorp (Russia), Miss Woolger (Belgium), Miss Dick (Britannia) and Miss Sullivan (France). (Illustrated London News Ltd/Mary Evans)

bill that week at Stratford Empire in London's East End. At the end of his 'turn', Robey had removed his stage make-up and motored across town to savour the atmosphere. As he recalled in his autobiography, he was unable to join in:

> I kept saying to myself, do they realise what has happened and what it means for the whole world? All the hat-wavers seemed in their early twenties, and they behaved as if perfectly confident that within a week or two the Kaiser would be on the run, Berlin in the hands of the Allies and peace would be secured for evermore. I reached home feeling more like a gloomy Dean than a Prime Minister of Mirth.[2]

Earlier, there was no sign of Robey's gloom being shared by West End theatre-goers. Playhouses and variety venues were as busy as ever with people enjoying the metropolitan theatrical delights. The original play of *Kismet* had just passed its 500th performance at the Globe. Topical revues were all the rage – *Hello Tango!* at the Hippodrome reflected the current tango craze; *The Passing Show* at the Palace, starring Basil Hallam performing his show-stopping 'Gilbert the Filbert' number, couldn't have been more up-to-the-minute when singer Clara Beck electrified the audience with 'I'll Make a Man of You'. Yet another lavish revival of *The Belle of New York* filled the Lyceum; and the big draw at the London Coliseum was revered actor Charles Hawtrey in a duologue, *The Compleat Angler*, heading a variety bill that featured female impersonator Bert Errol.

'The public are certainly not minimising the seriousness of the situation, but gloom is not predominant,' noted an *Era* reporter after testing the patriotic temperature inside these theatres. Indeed, the 'going mad' syndrome (or what George Bernard Shaw dismissed as 'war delirium') was liable to break out at any point during shows. The audience 'jumped to its feet' midway through the variety bill at the London Pavilion when the orchestra struck up 'Rule, Britannia!' and the curtain rose to reveal a gigantic Union Jack hanging from the flies, before everyone settled down to welcome Marie Lloyd's return from her recent American trip. At the London Opera House in Kingsway, upbeat patriotism stopped the show in its tracks when a baritone gave a hearty rendering of 'Tommy Atkins'. At the New Middlesex, 'cheering enthusiasm' greeted the introduction of a hastily mounted tableaux representing the Triple Entente: when Victor Brevy sang 'La Marseillaise', the curtain rose on a female figure bearing the French Tricolore, with the British and Russian flags behind her and a gallant Gaul grasping the hand of a Russian soldier.[3]

Beyond the metropolis, cheering in theatres must have sounded like the collective voice of Britons about to deliver the Kaiser a knockout blow. At Brighton's Theatre Royal, the appearance of a chorus of French soldiers in the tour of *Oh! Oh! Delphine* aroused 'great enthusiasm'. In *A Lucky Miss*, just across the road at the Hippodrome, Florence Wray was 'cheered loudly' when she ended 'Land of Hope and Glory' to a background of the flags of the Allies. On the other hand, a *Manchester*

*Evening News* journalist calling at local theatres detected an apprehensive 'nervous tingle' in the air:

> It was variously shown in the quiet demeanour of some audiences, the patriotic outbursts at places where the National Anthem was played at the outset of the performances, the anxious scanning of special editions of the newspapers during the show, and the somewhat half-hearted laughter where merriment usually reigns supreme. [4]

Caught on the hop between the traditional summer break, when many theatres closed for up to six weeks, and the general reopening for the autumn season, the entire theatre industry seemed to experience a nervous tingle over the next few days, even when the Chancellor of the Exchequer, David Lloyd George, assured a hastily arranged meeting of representatives from most national industries that the government would 'enable the traders of this country to carry on business as usual'.[5] His intention was to calm the markets. Instead the 'business as usual' mantra triggered what *The Stage* described as the usual 'alarmist tendency' amongst theatre managements fearing a sudden drop in box office receipts. Will it really all be over by the Christmas pantomime season? Nobody knew. Some were in favour of suspending 'theatre as usual' altogether for a month or so, a not unreasonable approach when so much investment in productions was at stake and many thousands of livelihoods faced an uncertain future.

By 1914, Edwardian theatre was not just a powerful cultural force: it was an integral sector of the national business environment – a fiercely competitive industry comparable in scale and annual turnover with many others in Britain. Commercial brand names of the great theatrical conglomerates such as Stoll and Moss were as well known as manufacturers such as Cadbury and Sunlight Soap. As early as 1906, an enterprise on the scale of the Moss Empires partnership with Oswald Stoll's company, running three-dozen theatres across Britain, including Stoll's flagship Coliseum in London, had become the largest theatre enterprise in the world.[6] At the top of the show business tree were interlaced networks of impresarios, theatre lessees, independent producers and actor–managements. In 1914, lucrative new touring circuits enabled old music hall hands such as Vesta Tilley and Marie Lloyd to command hundreds of pounds a week, equivalent to footballers' salaries today. West End stars and big draw variety turns excepted, most jobbing actors and performers often lived a precarious existence between contracts. Lower down the scale, ordinary theatricals might be lucky to take home 35*s* a week, out of which lodgings would have to be found on tour – and no rehearsal pay either. In 1914, Britain was criss-crossed with an extensive network of venues catering for all classes of theatre-goers, albeit physically separated by their stalls, circle and gallery construction, but these state-of-the-art neo-classical palaces invariably existed side by side with less-than-glamorous, low-grade local theatres of the type described by Robert Roberts in his autobiographical account of Edwardian industrial Salford, where touring actors seemed like aliens:

> We watched the small-part actors with cheroots swaggering through the stage door in lush coats, astrakhan collared, and were amazed to discover through the matriarchs (who knew everything) that many of them owned but a single shirt apiece or one pair of socks.[7]

The full story of British theatre during four years of war includes these threadbare thespians as well as the glitzy charmed circle of famous stars: everybody, men and women, young and old, had a role to play at all levels, from the great theatrical knights and powerful impresarios to humble backstage staff. Huge numbers of theatre workers willingly rushed to answer Kitchener's various calls to enlist, and either fought at the Front, died in action or were wounded. As a true war economy developed, no aspect of the entertainment industry remained untouched. Theatres in cities and towns, large and small, experienced an entirely new buzz of activity as a consequence of the emergency, whether it was for recruitment, raising charity funds, billeting soldiers, entertaining the wounded, spreading propaganda, asserting national pride, announcing news from the battlefields, or bolstering the morale of the civilian population. Pit orchestra musicians, songwriters, scene-shifters, designers, wig-makers, electricians, make-up suppliers, booking agents, theatre managers, front-of-house ushers, singers, dancers, chorus girls, variety turns, concert party artists, seaside pierrots ... they all found themselves embroiled in 'the most popular war this country ever engaged in'.

Disruption to 'business as usual' occurred immediately. On day one of war the government took over all rail transport: the special three-quarters fare concession for touring theatrical companies was cancelled, along with free trucks for transporting scenery. State control of the railways was vital for the movement of troops and munitions; but the economic viability of a large chunk of British theatre also depended on the efficiencies of the rail system. In August 1914, *The Era* listed thirteen separate touring circuits, ranging from the mighty Moss Empires, with thirty-seven theatres, to the smaller Midlands-based Kennedy Circuit, with seven. Even during the quieter 1914 summer holiday season, 119 touring productions and sixty-four concert parties were on the road. In 1913, the Great Western Railway alone carried more than 89,000 theatre and music hall passengers. For theatrical traffic between cities and towns to reach the following week's engagement it was quite normal to travel enormous distances by rail, usually on Sundays. Inevitably, the new timetable havoc signalled panic amongst those manning the levers of finance in the boardrooms of the touring circuits, concerned that productions could be cancelled, theatres might go 'dark' and box office receipts dry up.[8]

With rail services delayed, diverted, suspended or requisitioned for troop movements, most travel arrangements during the first months of war met with so many unforeseen difficulties that *The Stage* advised artists to avoid the usual cross-country Sunday trek and make a point of setting off as early as possible after the Saturday night performance, 'even though considerable delay is inevitable at changing points'. *The Era* urged managements to think ahead and invest in new technology:

Actor–aviator
Captain Robert
Loraine accepted a
commission in the
Royal Flying Corps
Special Division.
(Author)

'Now is the time to test the utility of the motor as a means of conveyance for theatrical productions. Various firms have plenty of petrol in store, and their motor lorries are capable of carrying any amount of scenery.' Inevitably, things constantly went awry: at Bradford Empire, the *Full Inside* company's plight typified a general 'show must go on' approach. When their sets and props were held up at Southampton, everyone went ahead and performed anyway: 'Without scenery to distract it, the audience more readily recognises the ability of the artists, and things go with a merry swing.' The *What Every Woman Wants* company was unable to get its truck of scenery from Birmingham to Bristol's Theatre Royal, so instead the cast appeared with stock sets provided by the theatre, which 'proved in every way satisfactory'.[9] Undaunted by logistical nightmares, actor–manager John Martin Harvey issued a defiant 'business as usual' statement when he opened his nationwide autumn Shakespeare tour at the Devonshire Park Theatre, Eastbourne, by taking out his biggest ever company, made financially viable by employing everyone on a profit-share basis. The tour also incorporated highly successful Sunday evening recruiting lectures.[10]

Although rail concessions for theatre companies were soon restored, breakdowns in transit arrangements continued for the duration. At the end of the 1914 summer season there were dozens of touring concert party troupes visiting holiday towns and coastal resorts, and these small-scale companies suffered the most from haywire rail schedules. *The Era* described how the *Blue Mouse* concert party arrived at Great Yarmouth to open at the Theatre Royal on a Monday, having come all the way from Darlington after being marooned between New Brighton and Tynemouth:

> On arrival at Liverpool en route, their truck of scenery was commandeered for military purposes. They opened at Tynemouth on Monday and all went well until the Wednesday morning. Then the company went to the theatre for a rehearsal but on arrival found the building in the possession of the military. From Tynemouth the company journeyed to Darlington on the Thursday but it was not until Saturday that they could get the props and scenery from the station to the theatre – owing to the lack of horses.[11]

Soon it was common to see notices outside provincial theatres warning of possible last-minute closures, often pinned up alongside war news. To make matters worse, 'business as usual' suffered even more when the new spectacle of uniformed recruits mobilising on city streets offered a far more exciting 'real' war experience than anything the stage could muster – and free of charge. In September, *The Stage* noted how in Aldershot, where more than 30,000 soldiers had mobilised, poor houses were the order of the day because crowds of soldiers and civilians filling the streets 'are so absorbed in the events happening in the war area that they are content in finding amusements from the scenes which take place in the streets at the present'. Another example occurred at Chelmsford, where: 'People find the windows of the newspaper offices engrossing points of interest, and the places of entertainment suffer.'[12]

Meanwhile, managements faced the twin prospect of actors and permanent staff suddenly rushing off to join the marching columns and their theatres being commandeered for military purposes. Leading actor and pioneering aviator Robert Loraine was one of the first to dash off when he accepted a commission in the new Royal Flying Corps Special Reserve. After three weeks training, he was flying reconnaissance missions at 2,000ft above the enemy lines, although by Christmas he was back home in hospital after a German bullet pierced a lung. He was awarded the Military Cross for bringing down a German Albatross in 1915.[13] Within days of war being declared, most of the employees at two Aldershot theatres – the Hippodrome and Theatre Royal – joined the Army, while the remaining stagehands, composed of Regulars, mobilised with their units. In Bognor, a tour of *Charley's Aunt* was terminated midway through a Saturday performance when producer–actor C. Lloyd Thomas, a reserve officer of the Royal Navy, received an urgent wire from the Admiralty to report to the nearest naval base. He left immediately for Portsmouth. In Doncaster, the Grand was one of many theatres in the country that closed in order to accommodate troops, while at the Palace, the ticket checkers left *en masse* to join the colours in a disastrous week that also saw top-of-the-bill act The Porcelains failing to appear because the rail company couldn't supply a truck for their scenery and props. On the Wednesday after war was declared, Devonport Hippodrome even lost an entire audience: a Bioscope screen was dropped during the performance showing an official order commanding all men to re-join their ships: There was an instant exodus from all parts of the house.[14]

What with 'free' military displays in the streets, random transport disasters and a steady loss of theatre personnel joining Territorial units or signing up for the British Expeditionary Force (BEF) in response to Kitchener's call for 100,000 men to enlist in the New Army, the main

*Above and opposite:* All-British products advertised in theatre programmes. (Author)

## TENNENT'S BRITISH LAGER BEER

### On Sale at the Bars of this Theatre.

theatrical managements issued a joint press statement urging the nation to keep theatres going:

> It is for the good of all that the public should, as far as possible, continue to patronise places of entertainment in order that the very large number of people in humble positions who are dependent upon this business for their livelihoods should not be thrown out of employment – and above all because they think it is essential for the good moral value of the people that 'business as usual' should be maintained throughout the country.[15]

By the end of September, expected economic meltdown in the theatre industry proved unfounded. After the sombre news of the BEF retreat from Mons and the Battle of the Marne, the beginnings of trench warfare and the publication of ever-lengthening casualty lists, business was, ironically, becoming better than usual, partly thanks to an ever-expanding khaki trade. In Chelmsford, for example, *The Stage* found that constant relays of Territorials and Regulars passing through the town and bivouacking overnight kept theatres busier than ever: 'At the Empire on Monday night they almost took sole possession of the hall, and all the artists had an uproarious welcome.' In seasonal Blackpool, takings at the Palace, the Grand and the Opera House benefited enormously from the constant churn of billeted troops, invariably looking for entertainment. Even without this box office boost, a statement from J.R. Huddlestone, general manager of the Winter Gardens, summed up the prevailing attitude: 'So long as there is a person in Blackpool to pay their sixpence admission I will keep my end up.'[16] In the same week, a poster appeared outside the London Pavilion signed by the manager:

Management has decided to maintain 'Business as Usual' for the following reasons:

1. An atmosphere of gloom will never help the nation, while rational amusement will do much to lighten its burden.

2. It enables a large number of staff and artistes to remain in employment, though the proprietors do not and may not benefit.

In wartime, as in times of peace, all are welcomed by the hospitable 'Pav'. It is hoped that all able-bodied young men, our former and most loyal patrons, will, unless prevented by other service to the State, promptly rally round the flag.[17]

There was no hospitality at the 'Pav' or anywhere else in the business for anyone with German nationality or a vaguely Teutonic-sounding name: theatre wasn't exempt from the Hun hatred gripping all sections of society. As the rounding up and internment of aliens gathered momentum, the

London County Council immediately refused to licence any theatre producer with German connections. Even those actors, performers, writers, musicians and other professionals who had become naturalised Britons felt obliged to prove they were not sworn enemies or part of the hidden network of spies secretly working for German victory. As soon as war was declared, Herr Schoenberger, conductor for *The Marriage Market* at the Grand Theatre, Blackpool, had his name changed on the programme to plain 'Mr', explaining to his own pit band musicians that he had lived in England for twenty-five years and had been naturalised for eighteen of them. Respected variety performers became enemy aliens overnight. The highest-paid circus act in the world, the German–Jewish Lorch Family of acrobats, were placed under arrest during their week in variety at Middlesbrough. Juggling genius Paul Cinquevalli, who had been among the acts invited to appear in the music hall's first ever Royal Command Performance in 1912, found himself completely ostracised and was forced to give up performing altogether after the tabloid press reported that he had been born with a Teutonic surname. In fact, he was Polish by birth.[18]

No wonder anglicising names, or changing them completely, was common: after all, even the Royal Family de-Germanised themselves, though not until 1917. For theatricals, however, it became an urgent survival strategy. Some posted disclaimer notices in the trade press:

In consequence of some misapprehension which seems to exist as to his nationality, Mueller of Mueller and Coyne, who is a natural born American subject, has decided to adopt his baptismal name of Miller. The entertainers will now be billed as Miller and Coyne.

Mme Van-Earle wishes it to be known that the name Van-Earle was originated by herself seven years ago merely for use on the stage, and is therefore purely Dutch made in England, and nothing to do with Germans or Germany. Until the present crisis is over the name will be written in one, leaving out the hyphen.

Notifying a name change was a priority for many theatre pit orchestra leaders who had adopted fashionable-sounding Viennese identities. Apart from public opprobrium, musicians were refusing to play with their 'foreign' colleagues, which is probably why this disclaimer appeared in *The Era*:

> Basil Hindenburg, director of the Torquay Municipal Orchestra, who is a natural born British subject, has decided to adopt his baptismal name of Cameron. For the future, therefore, he will be known as Mr Basil Cameron.

National paranoia about German spies was reflected in *The Man Who Stayed at Home*, which opened at the Royalty Theatre in December 1914. (Author)

A call to arms in the programme for *The Man Who Stayed at Home.* (Author)

One of the ugliest anti-German denunciations was issued by James M. Glover, musical director at the Theatre Royal Drury Lane and composer of jingoistic pantomime songs such as 'We Mean to be the Top Dog Still':

There is one thing that the war will finally shuffle off the British earth, and that is the German or Anglo–Viennese band, and any English musician who will again pass himself off as a 'foreigner' of this description deserves a slow, lingering death to the music of all our opponents' National Anthems played out of tune. It is thought that the easy accessibility of securing posts in English orchestras was not an unimportant vehicle for wholesale espionage.[19]

Patriotism didn't always tip over into Hun-hatred. Veteran music hall star Charles Coburn, whose signature song was 'The Man Who Broke the Bank at Monte Carlo', pleaded with colleagues to tone down their attitude to foreign artists:

> I think it is up to us to prove that we belong to a nation of sportsmen, by making their lot as little irksome as we possibly can, both by refraining from irritating comment, and by using our best endeavours to see that the public does not visit upon them the consequences of actions for which they are in no way responsible.[20]

Nevertheless, the introduction of the Trading with the Enemy Act in September 1914 sparked finger-pointing attacks in the press about royalties paid to composers of sheet music from West End shows ending up in German bank accounts. The English language production of *The Chocolate Soldier*, with music by the Viennese composer Oscar Strauss, came under attack, as did *The Cinema Star*, composed by Jean Gilbert (alias Hamburg-born Max Winterfeld). In fact, the outbreak of hostilities brought the regular traffic of plays and musicals between Berlin and London to a halt, ending a long-standing two-way relationship that had helped to shape Edwardian musical theatre. Any 'German' shows still remaining were quickly camouflaged with new titles or the names of composers deleted from programmes. One musical of 1914 at the Lyric Theatre, *Mam'sell Tralala*, also by Jean Gilbert, was revived in 1915 as *Oh! Be Careful*.[21]

As a patriotic alternative to the high-quality Berlin-based Leichner stage make-up used for decades by almost everyone in the acting profession, enterprising London costumier Willy Clarkson came up with his own thoroughly British greasepaint, advertised in theatre programmes and magazines as 'Goulding's Glarko'. Before long, Boots the chemists

German stage make-up was rapidly replaced by all-British brands. (*The Stage/ The Era*)

sold their own 'All-British' brand, with every stick carrying a donation to theatre charities. *The Stage* responded by listing the locations of Boots' stores, so that touring theatricals would know where to purchase supplies.[22]

There's no doubt that the uncertainty triggered by the new domestic wartime environment also brought out the creative best in theatre folk: as supporters of charities, encouragers of recruitment and as volunteers for service. The first theatrically connected West End recruiting centre since Wyndham's staged *An Englishman's Home* in 1909 was opened at the newly built Little Theatre, just off the Strand. Before anyone had seriously engaged with the enemy, an actors' corps of special constables was formed in London at a meeting at the Playhouse Theatre convened by actor–manager Cyril Maude. More than thirty actors signed up, with hours of duty arranged around their theatrical work, and each actor–constable was issued with a badge, a whistle and a baton. George Robey, well over military age, was among the first to join the Volunteer Motor Transport Group (Group II, City of London) with the honorary rank of lieutenant, meeting BEF soldiers arriving from all corners of Britain at Paddington, Euston or King's Cross and conveying them in lorries to Waterloo or Victoria for the train to carry them from Blighty to the fighting lines. Later, when the wounded started to return, Robey found the work increasingly harrowing:

I don't think any of us at home knew the sort of experience our soldiers had been through until the men of the first army came home on leave. Even then, it wasn't what they said that told us of the inferno they had come from. It was the look in their eyes – a haunted look. They would crack their jokes; they would come to the theatre and music hall and laugh with the rest of the audience – but their eyes told things that lips could not or would not tell.

This transport service, and an all-night buffet, was entirely provided for by voluntary gifts of money, most of it raised through Robey's all-star

Sunday evening concerts at the Coliseum – usually with an auction tacked on – which raised enough cash to keep the buffet going right up to the end of the war.[23]

Actors volunteered for military service well before *The Era* described 'actor–warriors' as ready-made for battle: 'The actor ought to make a smart soldier. He is alert, intelligent, habitually obedient, and essentially energetic.' Theatrical producer Leslie Owen even arranged a special company for actors in the 11th Battalion of the Royal Fusiliers. Before training began Owen joked: 'We start rehearsing on Friday and open in about ten or twelve weeks on a tour, the length of which is impossible to estimate, and finishing at Berlin. There will be no nights out and no half salaries.'[24] On 16 September, *The Era* also announced the formation of an actors' 'pals' corps:

> Lord Kitchener is in favour of raising battalions of men of individual professions and bound together by their calling. It is the obvious duty of the theatrical profession to supply such a corps. Actors of serviceable age who are medically fit are invited to join. Will those ready to do their duty to their King, their country, and for the glory of their profession apply to Mr Cyril Maude at the New, or to Mr Gerald du Maurier at Wyndham's Theatre.[25]

By the end of 1914 more than 600 'actor–warriors' had joined up, another 200 were in the United Arts Corps; and these figures do not include variety artists and musicians or backstage and front of house staff. In mid August, the first theatrical agent to join up was Frederick Malone, who had worked on the halls as a sword swallower under the name 'Chevalier Clicquot'. As he spoke several languages, Malone was made an interpreter and dispatch rider – supplying his own motorcycle. At the age of 53, music hall performer Leo Dryden – the 'Kipling of the Halls' and stepfather of Charlie Chaplin – volunteered for service, as did staff members from *The Era* and *The Performer*.[26]

Without any prompting, theatre professionals soon became the leading force in the immense voluntary effort sweeping the country. The speed with which theatrical charities of every size and description immediately sprang into action was phenomenal, with new ones regularly emerging as the war progressed. On the day hostilities broke out, Marie Lloyd vowed to provide 'creature comforts' for 'our London Lads in Khaki' by proposing to, 'invite my brother and sister artistes to co-operate with me in giving their services (and this I know they will do willingly) to organise a series of matinees and evening performances at our leading West End variety theatres'. Almost overnight, charity matinees, benefit performances, appeal concerts and on-stage auctions became part of the theatrical environment. Actors raised money by selling their publicity postcards; variety artists sold sheet music of their most popular songs. Actor–manager John Martin Harvey and his actress wife, Nina de Silva, even offered their summer cottage at Bonchurch in the Isle of Wight to the authorities as a war hospital. The house was the first on the island to fly the Red Cross flag.[27]

When, on 2 September, *The Era* established its own War Distress Fund (motto: 'Collect as much as you can, and pay out as quickly as possible') to collate donations from charity performances and provide immediate assistance to those in the profession, actress–producer Lena Ashwell was appointed chair of the committee determining the recipients of support. Ashwell, together with actresses Decima and Eva Moore and Eve Haverfield, had already established the Women's Emergency Corps (eventually expanding it to fifteen branches across the country) to channel the skills of 'all women trained in any capacity'. At the same time, Ashwell was one of the first to suggest a national scheme for professional actors to entertain the troops, with 'every camp its own theatre', though it was not until early 1915 that her Concerts at the Front brainchild came to fruition. Charitable and voluntary work was often the only direct way that women could support the war effort. One individual initiative came from actress Emily Willard, who founded an Actresses' First Aid and Nursing League, providing four beds for wounded men at her home at

Cast members of *The Country Girl* at Daly's Theatre engaged in making mittens and mufflers for soldiers pose for a publicity shot during a rehearsal break. (Illustrated London News Ltd/Mary Evans)

## PUT THIS PROGRAMME IN YOUR POCKET

TAKE it home. Stand it on your mantelpiece, where you will be sure to see it in the morning. Let it remind you that your duty is to help your country by saving all you can — every day — and by investing all you save in —

# NATIONAL WAR BONDS

### At any Money Order Post Office or Bank

Theatre programmes were soon being used to promote the first War Bonds issue. (Author)

19 Platt's Lane, Hampstead. *The Stage* described how an actress touring in *The Queen Mother* found time to help wounded soldiers and sailors by sending mufflers, bed socks and slippers knitted and crocheted by herself and members of the company to local committees and the Daily Sketch League, and how she also kept herself busy by autographing postcards, the entire proceeds from which (just under £15 in three weeks) were sent to the National Relief Fund.[28]

Meanwhile, the dramatic and variety stages mobilised to raise the national spirit. On the night war was declared, Frank Benson's annual Stratford-upon-Avon Shakespeare Festival company immediately cancelled *The Merry Wives of Windsor* and substituted *Henry V*. This was not done, Benson explained, simply to 'encourage a Jingo feeling', though, as *The Stage* reminded him, the play depicts the defeat of the French, 'which is scarcely paying a compliment to our allies across the Channel.'[29] The day after first night, Benson and company took part in a recruitment drive in nearby villages. In London,

The lavish restaging of *Drake* at His Majesty's, one of the first overtly patriotic West End productions of the war years. (Author)

Sir Herbert Tree fell in smartly by hoisting the flag at His Majesty's Theatre. In the days when actor–managers reigned supreme the 'Chief', as he was known to his staff, staged lavishly realistic Shakespeare productions and dramatic spectacles at this grand playhouse, where he also lived.

None were more lavish, more spectacular, more realistic or more patriotically inclined, than his 1912 production of *Drake*, by Louis Napoleon Parker. Tree immediately set about restaging it, after cancelling a planned production of *David Copperfield* and announcing that he would play the title role himself. Tickets were snapped up at 'popular prices', all profits going to the Prince of Wales's Fund, specially earmarked for injured theatre professionals. The cast volunteered to accept reduced rates; Phyllis Neilson-Terry, as Queen Elizabeth, donated her entire salary. Arriving audiences were met with a poster proclaiming:

> It is hoped that the public will, as far as possible, support the theatres during this period of stress. By doing so they will keep in employment a vast number of men and women: *Drake* alone affords employment to over 400 people.

An *Era* reporter captured the atmosphere on opening night (17 August 1914):

> During the intervals the audience, from gallery to stalls, were to be seen standing and singing together the national anthems of the Allied forces, while at the impressive scene of Drake's final triumph the crowded gathering joined the company singing God Save the King. It was essentially a patriotic night.[30]

By December 1914, *Drake* had raised more than £2,000, split between the Prince of Wales's Fund and the Actors' Benevolent Fund. For Tree, August and September were action-packed. *Drake* was followed by a revival of *Henry V*, which he claimed, 'voices the national spirit of the time'. He supplied the text of a short play (*The Ultimatum: Or Every Man Has His Price*) for *King Albert's Book*, a tome published by the *Daily Telegraph* at Christmas to pay tribute to the Belgian King and raise funds for Belgian refugees. Alongside British dramatists Arthur Wing Pinero, Arthur Henry Jones, J.M. Barrie, George R. Sims and Alfred Sutro, Tree was a signatory of the 'Authors' Declaration' of September 1914 (a product of the new War Propaganda Bureau) with its lofty morale-boosting manifesto aiming 'to maintain the free and law-abiding ideals of western Europe against the rule of "Blood and Iron" and the domination of the whole Continent by a military caste.'[31] Another signatory, actor–manager, producer and playwright Harvey Granville Barker, brought the year to a close by directing an epic stage version of Thomas Hardy's *The Dynasts* at Lena Ashwell's Kingsway Theatre. This vast verse drama chronicling the Napoleonic wars received critical acclaim for its innovative staging, with the battle of Waterloo taking on a special resonance when the nation was once again battling across the Channel. Barker's achievement stands out because the production avoided Tree's overt nationalism at a time when every other West End playhouse was presenting either lightweight fare with a patriotic flavour or blatant military tub-thumpers. Two weeks into the conflict, *The Era* had urged writers of war plays to avoid the tendency to 'boastfulness and brag':

> The public will resent flippancy and chauvinism as much as weakness. They are in a serious, savage temper, and after the present strain has become customary, it may after all, do, as Mr Gladstone did on an occasion of great mental pressure – go and see a funny or sensational piece: not a military one.[32]

Inevitably though, crowd-pleasing 'boastfulness and brag' flowed naturally into variety bills and revues, as if writers and composers had been preparing drawers full of patriotic sketches and songs in anticipation of war breaking out. A patriotic scene was immediately added to the revue *How D'Ye Do?* at Richmond Hippodrome, 'with all of the Allies represented, including Colonial contingents'. The Palladium programme was changed to include *Gentlemen of the King!* – a 'patriotic military episode'. The Moss Empires circuit sent out a hurried tour of *Our Allies* starring quick-change comedienne Liane D'Eve singing 'Tommy and Jack Will Soon Be Marching Back', Belgian tenor Vanni Dua, and a 'pageantry of war weapons' created by 'our Russian ally' Zakaree Ermakov (whose real name was Henry Gibson, an Australian-born circus performer).[33] At the London Opera House, C.B. Cochran slotted in *England Expects* by Seymour Hicks and Edward Knoblauch, in which a group of slackers were transformed into fighting men who end up triumphing in the trenches and waving the Union Jack while Esmé Berenger recited Rudyard Kipling's 'England's Answer'. *For France*, by the novelist Draycot M. Dell, a new dramatic sketch set in a farmhouse in Alsace at the end of the Franco–Prussian War, was presented simultaneously at the London Pavilion and the Hippodrome, Manchester. A quick addition to the Victoria Palace variety bill was a poem entitled 'Joan of Arc's Appeal to the British Nation', spoken by actress Quetta Maude clad in a suit of chain mail and hastily written by no less a figure than the Very Reverend Monsignor Robert Hughes Benson, the son of the previous Archbishop of Canterbury. On the same bill, alongside Val A. Walker ('The Wizard of the Navy') escaping unscathed from a metal submarine submerged in a glass water tank, Phyllis Dare introduced one of the great recruiting songs of the entire war, 'Your King and Country Want You'. 'Miss Dare appeals strongly to the patriotic sentiment and it will certainly not be her fault if recruits are lacking for Lord Kitchener's second army,' wrote a *Stage* reviewer stirred by a lyric urging young men to forgo boyish pursuits in favour of manly fighting.[34]

How many young men volunteered when prodded by 'Oh! we don't want to lose you but we think you ought to go / For your King and Country both need you so' is impossible to know. But as the need for more men to sign up became a national emergency, variety performers such as Dare, Vesta Tilley, Marie Lloyd, Hetty King and Ella Shields found new roles as supreme mistresses of recruitment, with an ability to turn their stage acts into the theatrical equivalent of revivalist meetings while employing their powerful on-stage magnetism to entice men from their seats to join the colours. Before compulsory service came in, most variety theatres held recruitment nights: the touring *What Ho, Tango!* company made a special patriotic effort on Fridays, when:

> The manager, Mr Jock Kirkpatrick, dons Scotch uniform in lieu of evening dress and sings a military number, and Tom Tutty, the principal comedian, makes an appeal for recruits. Last week at Stoke-on-Trent thirteen men from the audience signed their papers on the stage, four sergeants from local headquarters making the necessary arrangements.[35]

One music hall act even took their recruiting effort onto the streets of London's East End:

> A band of lady music hall artistes, The Red Heads, appearing at the Stratford Empire, formed themselves into a band of recruiting officers. They approached likely recruits in the streets, and, if successful in persuading their quarry to join the colours, accompanied them to the nearest recruiting office.

The ladies secured more than fifty recruits and received a letter of gratitude from the War Office.[35] In addition to recruitment, by the end of 1914, no variety bill, revue, concert party show or pantomime was complete without a patriotic overture and at least one of the full-throttle jingoistic airs being rushed onto the market, many of them composed by highly skilled songsmiths steeped in the music hall tradition and well-versed in the art of creating catchy melodies with easy-to-learn lyrics designed for mass choral participation. Official War Office recognition of popular theatre songs as an aid to recruitment had in fact come in a letter to the main variety managers. Signed by Captain Thomas Whiffen and sent at the end of August 1914, it read:

Dear Sir, Mr Harold Begbie's well-known verses 'Fall In!' have been set to music, and the object of this letter is to invite your cooperation in arranging if possible for the song to be incorporated in your programme, and in others controlled by you, with a view to encourage enlistment. The song is published in conjunction with *The Daily Chronicle* and the profits from the sales are given to the Prince of Wales's Fund.[36]

The eminent British composer Sir Frederic Cowen provided marching music to Begbie's lyric, with its guilt-tripping sentiment:

Is it naught to you if your country fall
And Right is smashed by Wrong?
Is it football still and the picture show
The pub and the betting odds
When your brothers stand to the tyrant's blow
And England's call is God's![37]

As entire communities watched men in khaki and blue marching off to war accompanied by such songs, the music publishing industry was poised ready to offer performers an endless supply of new ones. Francis and Day revised 'Now, are we all here? – Yes!' with special new war verses and promoted a long list of songs 'already arranged for the stage', including 'Hullo There! Little Tommy Atkins' and 'Come and be a soldier'. Frank Howard Ltd's 'Here's to the Day! (we've got a mailed fist, too)' was advertised in the theatrical press as 'specially written for the crisis'. Star Music rushed out band parts for 'Boys in Khaki Boys in Blue' by Arthur J. Mills and Bennett Scott (who came up with 'Take Me Back to Dear Old Blighty' in 1916). Feldman's not only had 'Sons of Our Sailor King' on offer but discovered an unexpected new lease of life for 'It's a Long Way to Tipperary' composed by music hall performer Jack Judge, which had already been turned into a popular success in 1913 by one the Edwardian stage's greatest chorus singers, Florrie Forde, but now became *the* marching anthem of the war.[38]

Music publishers were quick to promote patriotic songs for theatrical performance. (*The Stage/ The Era*)

A youthful Ivor Novello. (Author)

Performed in theatres everywhere, 'Till the Boys Come Home' (later changed to 'Keep the Home Fires Burning') was an instant hit. (*The Era*)

One talented young composer wanted to create something different. From his tiny flat on the top floor of the Strand Theatre in the Aldwych, overlooking the Gaiety Theatre, the relatively unknown David Ivor Davies, later known as Ivor Novello, dreamed up a haunting melody that became an instant hit and has remained the most evocative song of the war period ever since. 'Keep the Home Fires Burning' brought the

21-year-old composer overnight fame and enormous wealth well before he wore the uniform of a flight sub-lieutenant in the Royal Naval Air Service and achieved success as a film actor, composer and writer of musicals.

With new patriotic songs being churned out by the day, Novello's mother, singing teacher Madame Clara Novello Davies, urged him to try writing one himself, after coming up with her own derisory effort – 'Keep the Flag A-Flying'. Ivor's response took several rewrites and some lyrical input from Lena Guilbert Ford, an American poet living in England and a friend of his mother. The result was one of the most popular songs of all time. Under the title 'Till the Boys Come Home', it was first performed at a Sunday concert at the Alhambra Theatre, accompanied by Ivor on piano. The audience went wild, immediately tuning in to the yearning melody and earnest message of hope for both those at the Front and those left behind. On the following day the publisher, Ascherberg, Hopwood & Crew, was inundated with singers

The song soon became the battle hymn of the Great War. (Bamforth)

desperate to perform it onstage. Before long the song had swept the country, and was eventually introduced to the troops retitled as 'Keep the Home Fires Burning' by Novello himself when he was in France in April 1915 as a member of one of Lena Ashwell's concert party troupes, by which time the *Daily Mail* was able to describe the song as 'The battle hymn of the Great War'.[39]

Herman Darewski's score for a new revue at the Hippodrome, opening on 16 November 1914 and starring Violet Lorraine and Harry Tate, consisted almost entirely of the kind of upbeat songs that Novello did not want to emulate, including 'Three Cheers for Little Belgium' and 'When We've Wound up the Watch on the Rhine'. Considering that the war itself had reached a grim stalemate, the title of the show, *Business as Usual*, was both apt and ironic. By Christmas of 1914, it wasn't all over as everyone had believed: at home, life was slowly but surely becoming as entrenched as it was on the Western Front. Yet in four months of uncertainty theatre had more than done its bit, with free entertainment for the ever-growing numbers of sick and wounded soon joining the charity matinee as a regular fixture, while more and more soldiers took advantage of half-price admission offered by West End and provincial managements to men in uniform.

At the end of the year, the first serious war-inspired drama did at least attempt to reflect a more sombre mood compared with the bragging patriotism dominating the stage so far. J.M. Barrie's thirty-minute one-act play *Der Tag, or the Tragic Man*, opened at the Coliseum four days before Christmas Day as the heavyweight item on a bill that included Fred Ginnett's Boy Army and Russian ballet stars Theodore Kosloff and Alexandra Baldina. Strange and dream-like, *Der Tag* portrayed the Kaiser as a soul troubled and having second thoughts about the horrors he has unleashed on the world. The house was full for the opening performance, with Chancellor Lloyd George in attendance. But it was a critical disaster: *The Observer* said it was a credit to Barrie's patriotic passions, 'but hardly to his art'. Coincidentally, the more creditable side of Barrie's dramatic art was on show at the same time across the road at the Duke of York's,

# A NEW NOTION.

### Patriotic—Cinematographic—Realistic—Dramatic.

# "FOR THE FLAG"

is the title of a forty-minute playlet in five scenes. Every minute is action. Every scene is realistic. Three scenes are played by Actors and Actresses "in the flesh," and the same Actors and Actresses link up the sequence of events on films taken within the last fortnight **in the actual fighting area in the north-east of France.**

The company, who include Miss Muriel Palmer and Mr. Harold Heath, the well-known players, have just returned from the Front, whither they went by special permits (the passports and authenticated datings are on exhibition), and the result is vivid in the extreme.

"FOR THE FLAG" contains many sensations, including the heroine's dive into a tank 24 feet by 12 feet, the hero's race for life in a motor car, the bombardment of a farm and its demolition by an explosion.

## SEE IT AT THE MIDDLESEX NEXT WEEK.

*All communications:* THE V.B.O., Ltd. (*Sole Agents*),
**26, CHARING CROSS ROAD, LONDON, W.C.**
Telephone: Regent 2926.

The multi-media *For the Flag* attempted to convey the reality of war onstage. (*The Stage*)

where *Peter Pan* was enjoying its eleventh Christmas season (with a 14-year-old Noël Coward playing Slightly).[40]

A novel form of war drama emerged in 1914. The multimedia *For the Flag*, which opened at the New Middlesex in time for Christmas, employed live actors combined with silent film footage of them in an actual fighting area in north-east France. It was advertised as containing 'many sensations', including the heroine's dive into a tank, the hero's race for life in a motor car, the bombardment of a farm and its demolition by an explosion. Authenticated travel documents were exhibited as proof that the actors had just returned from France. Audiences thrilled to the wrecking of a Zeppelin and ignored the improbable plot. But one reviewer, noting that real war 'is a grim business', was unconvinced by such 'gallant footlight victories.'[41]

Meanwhile, pantomime audiences needed no encouragement to join in 'Till the Boys Come Home', although 'Sister Susie's Sewing Shirts for Soldiers' and 'Tipperary' were this year's most popular panto singalongs. Even in Cinderella-land or atop Jack's beanstalk, the war was never far away; but it was a fake footlights war avoiding any of the grim business that 'our boys' serving at the Front had experienced. At Drury Lane, *Sleeping Beauty Beautified* featured an army of toy soldiers and a Puck-like character in khaki singing 'Won't You Join the Army' backed by an orchestra conducted by the Hun-baiting James M. Glover. On Boxing Day, *The Times* noticed a strong colouring of khaki in the front rows intently watching the toy army onstage, but heard less noisy cheering and joining in than usual: 'The fact is "the boys" have taken themselves and their choruses to another front.'[42]

# 2

## 1915

### Khaki in the stalls, actors in the front line

Monday, 4 January 1915. Theatre Royal Drury Lane. 10.30 p.m.. The curtain has just come down on *Sleeping Beauty Beautified*. Within minutes the stage door flings open and the leading lady rushes out ahead of the rest of the cast. If Ferne Rogers looks flustered as she hails a cab, then it's only to be expected; she is starring in London's most spectacular pantomime and has just been forced to resign. Why? Because she likes Germans.

Earlier, the family audience roared with laughter when the chorus lined up as toy soldiers burlesquing a battle. They knew nothing of a backstage battle that threatened to close the show that night until two days later when news leaked out about the entire cast turning ugly because the American actress playing Beauty had been saying nice things about Germans. A round robin drafted by leading comedian George Graves (he performed the sibilant sing-a-long 'Sister Susie's Sewing Shirts for Soldiers' in the show) was delivered to theatre manager Arthur Collins complaining that Rogers had expressed so many pro-German sentiments

Ferne Rogers: sacked for saying nice things about Germans. (Author)

that the company would go on strike if she remained. Collins gave Rogers her marching orders; and the following day Nancy Buckland, the understudy who had been playing Zizi the dairymaid, stepped into Beauty's shoes.[1]

Rogers was on the next sailing to New York, abruptly ending a successful London career that had recently seen her feature in *By Jingo If We Do!*, ironically, a revue shot through with anti-German jokes. She was soon busy on Broadway again and in February found time to write an open apology in an American magazine addressed to her former Drury Lane colleagues. Yes, she had German ancestors. Yes, she trained with a German opera company. Yes, she was contrite about her tactlessness:

> When I started rehearsals at Drury Lane I found that apart from the pantomime itself, the only topic discussed was the war and unless I chose to allow myself to be considered tongue-tied I had to discuss the war in common with others, for there was nothing else being talked about.[2]

At a time when it was almost treason to say a good word about the enemy, Rogers' experience opens a chink on the feverish backstage atmosphere pervading every theatre in wartime Britain. As professionals settled into a new form of theatrical life, sharing stories about Germans, discussing rumours filtering through from the battle lines and exchanging news about colleagues in the trenches, or simply moaning about irksome problems brought about by the daily grind of war, dominated dressing room chit-chat. In early January an editorial in *The Stage* full of admiration for the 'cheerful valour' with which the work-a-day world of theatre 'carries on under many circumstances of discouragement' sat alongside gossipy backstage snippets in the paper's much-pored-over 'Actors and the War' column. *The Stage* was essential weekly reading in the profession, as were *The Era* and *The Performer*, but 'Actors and the War' provided a lifeline between dressing room and battleground. Today, the column reads like an online chatroom – a quick fix for anyone wanting to find out who had joined the colours and what they were getting up to. Having swapped stage costumes for real tunics, former theatricals sent postings from training camps in Britain or bases 'somewhere in France'; others requested supplies of stage make-up, old props, scripts or costumes to be used in the emerging front-line concert party entertainments. In early 1915, one actor wrote about being amazed to find his voice projection skills newly employed as a barracks square drill instructor. Former variety artist Bert Bray (now Gunner J. Jones) wanted ex-colleagues to know that he was laid up in Stanley Hospital, Liverpool, with concussion caused by a German shell. In January, there was news that Lieutenant Richard Damart, former lessee of the Criterion Theatre and a West End and Broadway leading man, had volunteered for service a month after war was declared, left for the Front two days later as a member of the Intelligence Department and was the first actor to receive the DSO for 'conspicuously gallant conduct in obtaining very valuable information under most difficult and dangerous conditions'.[3] When stage professionals began using the column to encourage enlistment, actor Richard Arundel wrote about training with the 3rd County of London Yeomanry as if it was a jaunty adventure involving galloping across Salisbury Plain and bivouacking under the stars:

> Where horses are one has never finished work, and night guards are pretty frequent, one every fourth night; but it agrees with me, I can recommend the life to other professionals as an excellent pick-me-up and tonic ... if you are prepared to rough it a little bit, join some regiment and you will never forget it.[4]

In May 1915, Private Wilson Roberts cajoled chorus members into joining the 19th Battalion London 'Pals' regiment established by Paul Murray, a booking manager for the all-powerful Variety Theatres Controlling Company syndicate:

> Surely they cannot say they are serving any purpose in this awful time dancing about and looking pretty on the stage, whilst their fellow

countryman are fighting and dying in the trenches in France and Belgium. Chorus ladies can certainly take the place of chorus men at the present crisis.[5]

Enlistment in Roberts' 'Pals' Battalion took place live onstage at the Oxford Music Hall in London: more than 100 new recruits were secured. Theatrical recruitment figures probably received another fillip when 'Actors and the War' readers learned that West End star Basil Hallam had resigned from *The Passing Show* to join the Kite Balloon Section of the Royal Flying Corps; though there's no mention that he was spurred on to enlist only after he and a friend, the aero engineer Granville Bradshaw, had left the theatre one night and found themselves in Shaftesbury Avenue surrounded by a group of 'young, stupid and screaming girls' who stuck white feathers in their lapels. Bradshaw recalled: 'When we extricated ourselves Basil said, "I shall go and join up immediately" – and he did, only to die in a parachute accident shortly afterwards.'[6]

You have to look elsewhere to discover the about-turn experienced by so many actor–soldiers discovering that military life was not the glorious adventure they had anticipated. Having signed up as a lance corporal in September 1914, promising American-born playwright and actor Harold Chapin found himself stationed at a Royal Army Medical Corps camp near St Albans surrounded by grumpy recruits kicking their heels. In one of many letters to his wife he wrote:

This Corps has been here five months now waiting and waiting and grumbling more and more the longer it had to wait till now it is in a very serious state of general hump – and to be among a lot of people who are half of them nursing grievances is rather depressing when one has quite enough to be humpy about without listening to others' imaginary grievances.[7]

Chapin didn't move off until March 1915, arriving at a base hospital in rural France, 'much nearer the firing line than I expected we would

HAROLD CHAPIN,
VIC–WELLS SHAKESPEARE CO.

PHOTO BY CLAUDE HARRIS.

Actor, playwright and theatre director Harold Chapin enlisted in the Royal Army Medical Corps in 1914. He was killed at the Battle of Loos. (Author)

be in the first few weeks, but far enough away for the war still to seem incredibly remote'. On the afternoon of 26 September, he was dead, shot in the head while rescuing a wounded man during the attempted British breakthrough at Loos.

Given his RAMC posting and former theatre connections, it's a fair assumption that Chapin knew about the trail-blazing New Year visit by husband and wife stage stars Seymour Hicks and Ellaline Terriss to the RAMC-manned No 14 General Hospital at Wimereux near Boulogne. The couple brought the first group of performers to entertain troops in France, billing themselves as:

**NATIONAL THEATRE AT THE FRONT.**
**A TENT, A ROADSIDE, A HOSPITAL – ANYWHERE.**
**THE PRICE OF ADMISSION IS OUR GRATITUDE TO YOU.**

Described by Terriss as 'a sort of New Year message for the soldiers', the pioneering ten-day visit was arranged by Hicks with War Office approval. After a big send-off at Victoria Station, the twenty-two-strong company, including pin-up actresses Gladys Cooper and Ivy St Helier, arrived at Boulogne with a piano and ten cars to ferry them around, stopping to perform anywhere there was a gathering of soldiers – by railway lines, in improvised halls, at hospitals and even in a fish market. 'We knew it would be rough work,' Terriss recalled. 'We gave our concerts in the travelling clothes we stood up in: we didn't mind, neither did the soldiers. We felt like old-time buskers, on the move and working all the time so the pathos of it all was forgotten, until later.'[8]

Immediately after Hicks and company departed from Wimereux Hospital, J.M. Hamber, a former actor, now on medical duties in the RAMC, sent 'Actors and the War' a first-hand account of the excitement among staff and patients generated by the visit:

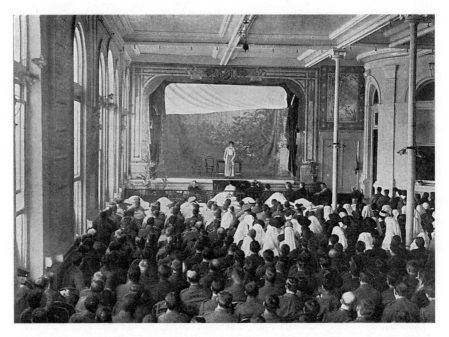

Ellaline Terriss singing 'Thank you for all you are doing,' to the soldiers and nurses in the hospital at Boulogne. (Illustrated London News Ltd/Mary Evans)

There are eight sleeping in my room, and at reveille this morning at 6am, we were all out of bed and dressing almost before the final notes of the bugle had ceased. 'Get up, Seymour Hicks is coming', and it was a beastly cold, wet, dark, dirty morning too! Well. They have for a few hours given us a welcome relief from the pain and sadness necessarily connected with a hospital like this. God bless 'em. We all do our work more cheerfully for their merry smiles.[9]

The National Theatre at the Front tour may have been short-lived, but as the first British actors to go trouping with the troops in France, Hicks and Terriss carved a niche in theatre history. Back in London, Hicks worked unstintingly for war charities for the duration, almost immediately going into rehearsals for a one-off charity performance of *The School For Scandal* at Covent Garden in aid of the Actors' Benevolent Fund. The King and Queen were in attendance, their first visit to a theatre since the outbreak of war.

At exactly the same time, from her actor–manager base at the Kingsway Theatre, Lena Ashwell was preparing to send over the first of her officially sanctioned YMCA entertainments for soldiers. Known as Concerts at the Front, the first contingent arrived in France on 15 February 1915 and gave thirty-nine concerts in fifteen days at YMCA huts and hospitals. Ashwell's ambitious beginnings eventually led to the creation of professional troop entertainment in several war zones, performing in tents, in acetylene-lit huts, in grim hospital wards, on ships at sea and at the bedsides of the dying: their first open-air concert was for the Army Veterinary Corps staff serving at the Forges-les-Eaux Horses' Hospital in northern France. They even gave public performances, one at the Folies Bergère in Rouen where, according to Ashwell's memoir, *Modern Troubadours*, local bigwigs were outnumbered by 'tier after tier of men in khaki'.[10]

Initially, in October 1914, Ashwell's attempts to gain War Office acceptance of the idea of entertaining troops by professional actors hit an official blank wall, despite backing from some Army high-ups and church luminaries. For Ashwell, the 'business as usual' mantra of the theatre world seemed 'absurd and selfish' in wartime; and, besides, she had 'always believed that theatre professionals ought to be on a par with the Red Cross and St John's Ambulance: 'for does not the soul of man need help as much as his body?' Fortunately, the Women's Auxiliary Committee of the YMCA, which had instigated the building of 250 YMCA recreation huts in rear areas, stepped in and Ashwell was invited to send a trial entertainment to Le Havre. She accepted the challenge – then hurried off to a wealthy friend for a cheque to cover the expenses. The experiment was still tentative because some in the YMCA hierarchy had qualms about associating with louche theatricals. Ashwell recalled how 'some expected us to land in France in tights, with peroxided hair, and altogether to be a difficult thing for a religious organisation to camouflage'. This led to strict conditions: no making use of the war to boost an actor's professional popularity; and every artist had to be personally known to Ashwell, who was charged with guaranteeing their conduct.[11]

By the time of the Armistice there were twenty-five separate Concerts at the Front troupes in France with a roll call of some 600 entertainers, more than half of them women. Alongside small roving companies, permanent parties were established in eight French towns and a group of actors dodged U-boats to put on shows in Malta, Egypt and Palestine. Repertory companies presented plays in Paris, Rouen, Havre, Boulogne and Calais. There were single entertainers as well and, at the end of 1915, a group performing dangerously close to the firing line. By January 1917, when a shortage of men had become an issue, Ashwell sent out parties composed entirely of women. Although women were by now moving into all sorts of roles previously reserved for men, this was considered a worrying innovation. Even so, Ashwell claimed success because:

> The chivalry of everyone was immediately aroused at the sight of these 'helpless' women; and throughout, touring parties of women only were the most successful, which can be easily understood if one can realise that it was an intense joy, as a man once said to me, 'to see a pair of slippers'.[12]

The original party of five included Ivor Novello, who had just written 'Till the Boys Come Home'. This group performed songs, recitations, and comedy monologues in a new cinema built at the YMCA's No 15 base in the Harfleur Valley, which was surrounded by so much mud that the company wore gumboots to negotiate the duckboards. In a room packed to suffocation, Ashwell described how the audience responded to hearing Novello's song for the first time, by then retitled as 'Keep the Home Fires Burning': 'The men seemed to drink it in at once and instantly sang the chorus, and as we drove away at the end of the concert, in the dark and rain and mud, from all parts of the camp one could hear the refrain of the chorus.'[13]

Hospital concerts could be disturbing; for the first time performers were coming face to face with the hideous consequences of the fighting,

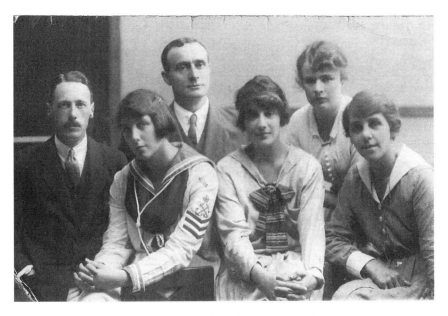

Members of a Lena Ashwell concert party bound for Egypt. (Author)

the shockwaves destroying the jingoistic veneer presented by the their own theatre industry at home. A nurse based at No 14 General Hospital, where the Hicks troupe had performed two months previously, described the arrival of an Ashwell concert party in mid March, just after the bloody engagement at St Elois:

> They gave a concert in the orderly room, as the men in hospital were too bad for us to have a concert in the hospital itself; but afterwards those kind people came into each ward and sang softly, without any accompaniment, to the men who were well enough to listen, and the little Canadian story-teller went round and told his stories to each man in turn as they were having their dressings done, the result being, that instead of a mass of suffering humanity having their wounds dressed, the men were happy through a time that is usually so awful ... it must have been a very trying job for them: the sights and smells are gruesome.[14]

In August 1915, the seventh Concerts at the Front party presented three one-act comic plays at base camps, written by the dramatist Gertrude Jennings. This was play-acting on the hoof, with no curtains, no dressing areas and a few sticks of furniture. Lighting consisted of candles on a packing case. What did that matter, claimed Jennings in the *Daily Sketch*, 'when we had audiences who thronged the halls, climbed upon benches and on each other's shoulders, pressed in at the doors, looked in at the windows and laughed and cheered as audiences had never done before!'[15]

Field Marshal Haig praised Ashwell's scheme as 'a source of endless pleasure and relaxation for many thousands of soldiers' and hoped that it would not collapse through lack of funds. That it didn't was entirely due to voluntary donations that met artists' out of pocket expenses while they were abroad as well, as travel, board and lodging costs. Ashwell faced more expense when Army Regulations ordered that everyone had to be in uniform: artists were fitted with modified YMCA uniforms. On top of all that, she also had to keep her own career on track and ensure that her Kingsway Theatre in London remained in profit. So while her companies were out in France, she embarked on an exhausting series of provincial theatre tours, often combining nightly theatre appearances with public meetings to raise cash. A behind-the-scenes committee based in New Bond Street drummed up all sorts of ingenious fund-raising ideas, including, in December 1917, a huge 'Petticoat Lane' fair at the Albert Hall, which raised £34,000, equal to more than £3 million today.[16]

Bringing a little bit of professional show business to France must have seemed like a great big pioneering adventure. However, a more informal entertainment structure was beginning to take shape in France by 1915, which eventually became institutionalised by the military authorities. These scratch concerts involved soldiers and sailors themselves, often gifted amateurs or former theatre professionals, and were inspired by popular forms of theatrical entertainment that everybody knew from their civilian lives. Later, big stars went out to the Front on morale-boosting missions, including George Robey, Harry Lauder and Leslie Henson; but self-organised concert parties were the mainstay.

For soldier–entertainers it wasn't just a killing war; it was a singing, dancing and laughing war, with shows staged either in the open air, in the growing network of field theatres, in hospitals, on board ships and at

In a concert on board a ship, sailors mimic Violet Lorraine and George Robey in the hit show *The Bing Boys are Here*. (Author)

Royal Flying Corps aerodromes. Recreation activities offered an escape from grimness and provided respite from long stretches of boredom. Concerts were essentially communal experiences, bonding irreverence and sentimentality with thoughts of loved ones left behind and nostalgic memories of shared nights out at theatres and music halls. Even the chalked-up signs at the junctions and corners of trench networks adopted well-known street names associated with West End theatres: you might be somewhere in France but passing along 'Shaftesbury Avenue' via 'Leicester Square'.

Songs from West End shows were imported by those lucky enough to own a compact portable wind-up gramophone. Soldiers on leave saw musicals and revues and brought shellac records of songs they had heard back to their units. Decca even promoted its sturdy portable Dulcephone player as 'Footlights at the Front – the Decca is Theatre, Music Hall and Concert Hall in one'.[17] Popular recordings included Violet Lorraine singing 'Three Cheers for Little Belgium' from the 1914 hit *Business as Usual* and comedian Harry Tate's rendition of 'Fortifying the Home Front'. But the demand was mostly for sentimental songs, especially 'If You Were the Only Girl in the World' from *The Bing Boys are Here*. *The Voice* magazine described how West End hit songs were heard in the most unlikely places:

> As one goes up to the trench at night and passes the last battered house where the road ends and the communication trench begins, a crack in the mud-plastered wall reveals a candle on a biscuit tin and two or three wearily lit faces listening to the strains of the latest revue. And somehow watching the rhythm of a waltz refrain bringing memories of happier days in London has a strangely heartening effect on the laden men stumbling on the cracked trench boards.[18]

Once organised entertainment took hold, performers scrambled around for costumes, sets and props, and slotted rehearsal time into their military duties; Putting on a show with whoever might be willing

There was a ready supply of new songs for camp concerts. (*The Era*)

Music publishers ensured that performers at home could respond to major events. (*The Era*)

## The Greatest Song of the Day.

# 'THE REPLY'

## Britain's Answer to the Lusitania Crime and Germany's Other Atrocities.

A remarkable song, full of contrasts. The forceful dignity of its words and the irresistible swing of its music invariably bring down the house. No Singing Act can afford to miss it.

As "THE REPLY" is published under the auspices of the Lord Mayor of London, and the entire profits donated to the Lord Mayor's Fund for "Lusitania" sufferers, no free copies can be issued, but Members of the Profession will be supplied at half-price—6d.

Get your copy to-day—it will be your greatest number.

If you are looking for 'unusual' Songs that will give individuality to your act, come in and hear some of our New Publications.

## HAL FRYER MUSIC CO.

11, Southampton Row, W.C.
(near High Holborn). 'Phone 1159 Museum.

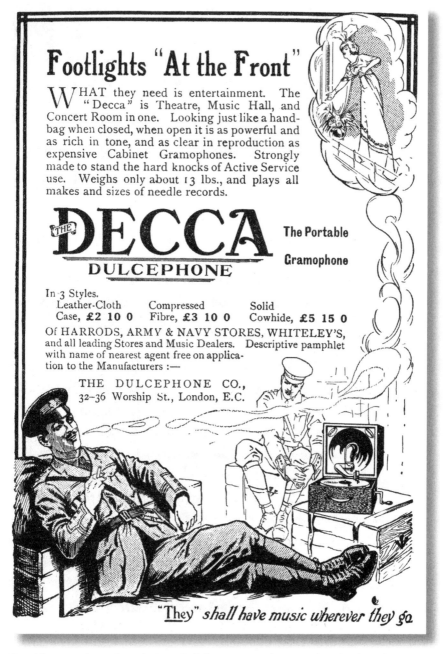

# Footlights "At the Front"

WHAT they need is entertainment. The "Decca" is Theatre, Music Hall, and Concert Room in one. Looking just like a hand-bag when closed, when open it is as powerful and as rich in tone, and as clear in reproduction as expensive Cabinet Gramophones. Strongly made to stand the hard knocks of Active Service use. Weighs only about 13 lbs., and plays all makes and sizes of needle records.

## THE DECCA
### DULCEPHONE

The Portable

Gramophone

In 3 Styles.

| Leather-Cloth Case, **£2 10 0** | Compressed Fibre, **£3 10 0** | Solid Cowhide, **£5 15 0** |
|---|---|---|

Of HARRODS, ARMY & NAVY STORES, WHITELEY'S, and all leading Stores and Music Dealers. Descriptive pamphlet with name of nearest agent free on application to the Manufacturers :—

THE DULCEPHONE CO.,
32–36 Worship St., London, E.C.

*"They" shall have music wherever they go.*

Portable gramophones brought West End show tunes to the Front. (*Land and Water*)

to appear also meant that rank divisions all but vanished. *The Fancies* of the 6th Division were in operation in France by the end of 1914, followed by the 4th Division's troupe, *The Follies*, in early 1915, both establishing a variety-style format that subsequently became almost universal at unit, divisional, brigade and battalion levels. Whether they called themselves *The Tonics*, *The Shrapnels* or *The Whizz-Bangs*, these troupes all mirrored concert parties and pierrot shows at home that would have been familiar to everyone. Comics mimicked well-known music hall sketches, such as Harry Tate's 'Motoring' routine, and sent up official ineptitude. Charlie Chaplin impersonations always went down well: a little tramp lookalike invariably featured at some point and everybody knew 'The Sun Shines Bright on Charlie Chaplin', described by the *Daily Mail* as 'The song that half the nation is singing'. In some respects these shows were a live equivalent of articles mocking the military brass and parodying contemporary issues in the trench newspaper *The Wipers Times*. Monologues, skits, singing and burlesques became the mainstay, but their emotional value was captured by Siegfried Sassoon:

> It wasn't much; a canvas awning; a few footlights … [the performers] were unconscious, it seemed to me, of the intense impact on their audience – that dim brown moonlit mass of men. Row beyond row, I watched those soldiers, listening so quietly, chins propped on hands, to the songs which epitomised their … longing for the gaiety and sentiment of life.[19]

Former theatre professionals naturally gravitated towards trench entertainment outfits. One of them was West End comedy actor Eric Blore, who ran the 38th Divisional concert party, *The Welsh Wails*, and became a Hollywood character actor after the war. Another was Private Ruben Winthrop of the Royal Field Artillery, who already had experience as a professional comedian in America. In later life, Winthrop changed his name to Bud Flanagan, became one half of the Flanagan and Allen double act, was the kingpin of the Crazy Gang and, in retirement, sang the theme song for the TV series *Dad's Army*. After seeing action at Vimy Ridge and being gassed, he joined the highly rated *Duds* concert party formed by members of the Liverpool 'Pals' Regiment, where his show-stopping act included impersonations of superior officers. But in 1915 he was in a typical small concert party, thrown together while on the move along various sections of the Front:

> We rigged up a tarpaulin as a backdrop in a field – no piano, only a banjo and paper and combs for accompaniment, and gave a really bright show, full of laughs, which lasted about an hour. The Colonel promised he'd get me a piano from somewhere and he kept his word. Within a day or two an old upright arrived. We were lucky in having a banjo player, who tuned it and later became the pianist. The shows improved.[20]

Inevitably, when costumes, sheet music or musical instruments were required, professionals turned to the 'Actors and the War' column in *The Stage*. Often the call went out for recycled 'ladies clothing'; old scripts were always in demand. When Rifleman H.C. Boreham of the 9th County of London Regiment (formerly the producer of *The Wedgwoods* concert party), appealed to readers for 'rags, sketches, or anything will do as long as they are workable after a few rehearsals', he also gave a first-hand description ('written in a dug-out') of the rough and tumble of an evening of sentimental songs and comedy monologues:

> You would be surprised to see our shows. We have secured a faded piano and a lot of black and white check stuff for draperies at the back, the lighting being supplied by motor lamps. Our dressing room (!) is shared by pigs and horses, to guard the 'props'! Of course, the perfume does not go well with greasepaint. This assorted company sometimes leads to disastrous results. Imagine a chap the other night singing 'I Hear You Calling Me' to the mingled accompaniment of squeals, grunts and strains on the piano. Poor chap, he's a decent voice too.[21]

Meanwhile, at home, on Whit Monday, the first seaside concert party season of the war was just getting under way in Colwyn Bay when two long-established companies came under attack. The Germans weren't responsible: hostilities came from locally based British soldiers in training who objected to artists apparently of military age appearing onstage. New recruits from the 1st Glamorgan Bantams, the 10th Gwent Battalion and the Cardiff City Battalion howled down *The Serenaders* at the Pier Pavilion with calls of 'try khaki on'. The soldiers, mostly former South Wales coal miners, then ran along the prom to the Arcadia Pavilion where, to shouts of 'smash the show', so many lumps of earth were hurled at the cast of *Will Catlin's Pierrots* that the manager had to be escorted to a nearby police station for his own safety. The performers protested: most of the artists were not eligible for military service anyway; some had been rejected when they volunteered; at least five artists who usually appeared were already in the ranks. Nevertheless, the theatres were forced to close for two nights 'for the public safety'.[22]

These were certainly odd times to be out of uniform in show business. In this pre-compulsory service period, actors, performers and theatre staff who might appear to be of military age were just as vulnerable to accusations of cowardly shirking as any other civilian, even though the industry was clearly doing its bit: by mid 1915, at least 1,000 theatre professionals had enlisted.[23] As the war rolled on, the pressure placed on artists to join up must have been intense, especially when more and more soldiers on leave, training in barracks or convalescing began filing into the stalls and asking why apparently able men onstage were escaping the hardships they had endured. Out and about on public view, the Tommy in uniform was revered; any young chap in civvies suspect. As the military historian Edward Legge noted at the time: 'The wearer of the uniform is the idol, the hero of the day; just as the laggard is frowningly regarded with chilling indifference, often mingled with disdain.'[24] Given the military mood music, theatre folk could hardly ignore the drumbeat of duty that accompanied it, especially if the pressure to get into uniform came from within the profession itself. A performer writing to 'Actors and the War', for example, suggested that managements should be forcing artists to join up:

> There must be scores of young men eligible for the Army working in various revues and musical comedies now running. To judge from advertisements in your columns there might easily be a battalion. If managers declined to engage any young men of military age unless he had been rejected by the authorities, it would no doubt help.[25]

Actor–manager John Martin Harvey, by now in his early fifties, wore the dashing stetson, neckerchief and riding breeches of the Legion of Frontiersmen to make a similar call when he opened his annual autumn tour at the New Brighton Winter Gardens by reciting the hymn 'Love for England' followed by his set piece encouragement to enlist, concluding with: 'The time has gone by when any young fellow of military age can walk about in civilian clothes and look khaki-clad heroes in the face.'[26]

Visible in the glare of the footlights, actors, performers and musicians of serviceable age walked a perilous tightrope. Just weeks after Ferne Rogers was sacked from Drury Lane for being nice to Germans, 31-year-old Godfrey Tearle, playing the naval hero in a revival of *The Flag Lieutenant* at the Haymarket, faced public derision during a performance when a woman in the stalls brandished a white feather at him. This humiliation came in the same week that the *Daily Express* put 'Five questions to men who have not enlisted', including 'Do you feel happy as you walk along the streets and see men wearing the King's uniform?' Tearle protested that an actor is 'the least fitted man in the world to become a soldier', but became one when he joined the Royal Artillery as a gunner, wearing the King's uniform until he was demobbed in 1919. Appearing in touring repertory, actor Clarkson Rose remembered facing feather branding on many occasions: 'It was an unenviable time for men like myself who looked fit but were not, for busybodies of the female sex went about presenting them with white feathers.' Rose had, in fact, volunteered twice but was rejected by medical boards for a suspected lung disease.

The Khakians – a typical Home Front concert party with military appeal. (Author)

Good-looking young musical comedy actor Jack Buchanan, appearing in a tour of *In the Trenches*, about a lonely soldier who never received a letter, lived in constant dread of the white feather treatment, despite being physically disabled. When full conscription arrived in 1917, he too was declared unfit for military service.[27] Eventually, even though it looked bizarrely out of place onstage, some actors wore khaki armbands or 'On War Service' badges to signal their non-slacker status. If audiences needed further assurance that they weren't watching laggards, managements inserted notices in programmes. The Haymarket Theatre's disclaimer was typical:

> All the male members of the cast and the members of the staff and the orchestra of the theatre have either served and been discharged from the Army or are ineligible for military service.[28]

By mid July 1915, when it was clear that purely voluntary recruitment would never provide the numbers of men required for an ever-expanding war producing ever-lengthening casualty lists for ever-diminishing territorial gains, the government passed the National Registration Act. All men between the ages of 15 and 65 who were not enlisted were required to register. From then on, it was so common for eligible-looking young actors to be greeted by loud hissing sounds from the stalls that *Punch* couldn't resist chiming in with a cartoon depicting a dresser telling a veteran actor making up to play Romeo: 'I wouldn't make yourself too young, sir, case they might get 'issing you for not 'listing.'[29]

Theatre-goers weren't exempt from these pressures. Notices appeared in foyers asking 'Why aren't you in khaki? You'll be wanted. Enlist at once', or 'Don't stand looking at this – go and help!' The entrance to the London Pavilion even displayed placards suggesting patrons of a suitable age should 'go and enlist before coming in'.[30] Theatres could also entrap men on leave if they were out of uniform. When Private Harold Carter arrived home after a tough time at Ypres, the first thing he did was to throw his muddy tunic in the wash tub, jump into clean civvies and

## National Service

I am desired by the Director-General of National Service to urge every man between the ages of 18 and 61 to place his services at the disposal of the State.

*(Signed)*

### GEORGE ALEXANDER

Department for dealing with Theatres, Music Halls and Entertainments

St. Ermin's Hotel, S.W.

When the National Service scheme was introduced, theatre programmes encouraged patrons to enlist.

Performers rallied the troops offstage as well as on. Music hall star Charles Coburn drums up recruits at the base of Nelson's Column. (Author)

queue with his girlfriend outside the local music hall, only to find a white feather thrust into his hand by a woman. Then, as soon as they were seated in the gallery, he received a barracking from a naval officer:

> No man should be out of uniform, he went on – if he was out of uniform he was nothing more than a worm and a skunk! He made me feel about as big as a worm, I just sat there, on my own, while people looked at me and I looked at them. I should like to have jumped up and told them I'd just come out of the trenches at Ypres, but I couldn't, I came out disgusted and went home.[31]

By the end of 1915, some 2 million men had volunteered. It is impossible to know how many joined up as a direct result of emotive appeals from the stage by the likes of John Martin Harvey or Marie Lloyd. The 'Queen of the Halls' had already imbued khaki with sex appeal during the Boer War with her risqué 'The Girl in the Khaki Dress' ('Khaki cuffs and collars, yes, and khaki 'dicky dirts'/And I've got khaki bloomers on underneath my skirts'). Fifteen years later, her wartime hit 'Now You've Got Yer Khaki On' transformed ordinary blokes into sexy heroes:

> Now, I do feel so proud of you, I do honour bright,
> I'm going to give you an extra cuddle tonight,
> I didn't like yer much before yer join'd the army, John,
> But I do like yer, cocky, now you've got yer Khaki on.

By contrast, Scottish comedian Harry Lauder's on-stage appeal was pecuniary rather than erotic – he started his act with an offer of 'ten pounds for the first recruit tonight'. Overall, Lauder claimed to have recruited 12,000 men, a figure that is probably close to the truth considering his extraordinary double-barreled campaign to reel in 'the scores of thousands of men in Britain who needed only the last quick shove to send them across the line of enlistment'. At his own expense and with War Office support, Lauder organised a recruiting band of

Scottish pipers and drummers and sent them across Britain, 'skirling and drumming the wail of war' all the way to local recruiting stations. Once there, he recalled how:

> the young fellows who weren't 'quite ready to decide' and the others who were just plain slackers, willing to let better men die for them, found it mighty hard to keep from going on the wee rest of the way that the pipers had left them to make alone! I felt like the Pied Piper!

While pipers wheeled in recruits, Lauder himself whizzed across the country on his theatre tours, invariably ending the act with a well-rehearsed lachrymose speech urging men to enlist:

> In the years to come, mayhap, there'll be a wee grandchild nestling on your knee that'll circle its little arms about your neck and look into your wrinkled face, and ask you: 'Did you fight in the great war, Grandpa? What did you do?' God help the man who cannot hand it down as a heritage to his children and his children's children that he fought in the great war.

Lauder was good news for recruiting officers, but bad news for pacifists. When a group of conscientious objectors paraded through the streets of London, he wanted to rush out from a theatrical lunch held to celebrate his charitable efforts and throw them into the Thames: 'Cutting their throats would be too quick for them,' he told his hosts. Thankfully, Lauder never got his hands on the actor Frank Pettingell, who in 1915 wrote and performed 'We Cannot All Be Soldiers (Men Who Are Left Behind)', a 'musical monologue' dedicated to the men who were unable to follow recruiting pied pipers for one good reason or another.[32]

We will never know how many undecided men were persuaded by Vesta Tilley's enticement powers: in one memorable week at the Hackney Empire in 1915 she is said to have single-handedly enlisted an entire battalion of 300 recruits, dubbed the 'Vesta Tilley Platoon'. Well before war broke out, Tilley was one of the highest-paid music hall stars, outclassing all the 'Beau Brummel' male impersonators who strutted the Edwardian stage in masculine attire. Hetty King wore a Jack Tar uniform and smoked a pipe when she sang 'All the Nice Girls Love a Sailor'; Ella Shields parodied Tilley's 'swell' Bertie character as 'Burlington Bertie from Bow'. But Tilley was already in a trouser-wearing, gender-swapping league of her own when war conditions suddenly gave everything that she had achieved onstage a new purpose, especially her routines skilfully designed for maximum audience participation. At the Palace Theatre, Manchester, for the week of 26 October 1915, she was first act on after the interval. The pit orchestra played a 'patriotic selection', including the anthems of the Allies. Then, dressed as a Tommy, Tilley marched onstage as if she had just arrived by train from the Front. With a backpack, a regulation rifle slung over her shoulder, a German spiked helmet in her hand and Flanders mud on her boots, she launched into 'Six Days' Leave'. Always a stickler for realistic detail, Tilley insisted on her

Harry Lauder with his recruiting pipe band. (Illustrated London News Ltd/Mary Evans)

backpack being the same weight as a real Army pack; she even mingled with troops at Victoria Station to observe exactly how returning soldiers handled their kit. After a quick change in the wings, she limped back in hospital blues for 'A Bit of a Blighty One', followed by 'Jolly Good Luck to the Girl that Loves a Soldier'. Then came her big finish: 'The Army of Today's All Right' (the War Office used this title for a poster asking for volunteers), during which she marched around accompanied by a chorus of real servicemen while singing 'We don't want to lose you, but we know you must go'. Then they all trooped through the auditorium with a column of converts in tow until everyone arrived onstage to be greeted by a real recruiting sergeant, with pen and official papers at the ready.[33] A *Manchester Guardian* critic watching Tilley in action recognised her charismatic allure but failed to link it with the reality that, like all wartime's showbiz pied pipers, she was effectively luring a percentage of her platoon to their deaths:

> Can the stage which is called legitimate show a fame which is so rooted in the consciousness of its own times? We doubt it. She is the most imitated of all performers on the stage and the most inimitable. She has created a whole school of stage art, and its practitioners, even the best of them, are, in comparison with her, deplorable.[34]

Theatres were not only magnets for recruitment. As 1915 drew to a close, no variety bill was complete without a Bioscope screening of war news clips, with titles such as *British and Belgian troops skirmishing in Flanders* or *Winston Churchill addressing military workers* bringing home something of what it was really like on the front line. On the night of 13 October 1915, the theatre industry itself received a reality check when the Germans brought front-line danger to the West End. At around 9.30 p.m., Zeppelin L15 drifted across Regent's Park, but the captain reserved his bombs until he was over the Strand, dropping the first at Exeter Street and the second at Wellington Street, close to the Lyceum, Strand, Gaiety and Aldwych

Vesta Tilley as a typical British Tommy on six days' leave. (Author)

theatres. Seventeen people were blown to pieces; many more seriously injured. At the Lyceum, the bombardment struck during the interval. Mary Davis, an actress appearing in the melodrama *Between Two Women*, was covered in falling glass in her dressing room. One patron, Lilian Weyman, recalled how she panicked when she couldn't find her brother, who had gone outside to get an interval drink at the Old Bell pub, just behind the Lyceum. It received a direct hit:

> I got to the street and what a dreadful sight. A broken gas main was flaring up from a huge crater and ambulance men were carrying stretchers of dead and wounded. I made my way back into the theatre again as it was useless to look for my brother in that hell and I knew that if he were still alive, he would come to look for me … I heard someone say 'Six men were killed at the public house at the corner' but fortunately my brother came to collect me.

At the Gaiety, directly opposite Ivor Novello's flat, the revue *Tonight's the Night* was in full swing when the bombs fell. While a packed house was enjoying songs by Paul Rubens (who wrote 'Your King and Country Want You' for Vesta Tilley), the door of the scene dock was blown in and near panic ensued. Comedian Leslie Henson, who was onstage at the time, said he became aware of the audience 'rising like a field of waving corn'. The musical director whipped the pit orchestra into one the show's liveliest numbers, so Henson leapt on a couch on the set and proceeded to jump up and down on it in time to the music: 'That brought laughter and gradually the audience recovered and took their seats,' he recalled. Backstage, a Gaiety electrician was killed and the cellarman had his left leg blown off. James Wickham, callboy at the Gaiety, and Billy, the pageboy, were posting letters in the Aldwych when the second bomb dropped yards from where they were standing; Billy was killed instantly and James had twenty-two pieces of shrapnel removed from his body in hospital. At the Aldwych, actor Sydney Hart was at the side of the stage watching Milton Rosmer speaking his lines in *The Prodigal*

*Son* when the explosions rocked the place, sending the audience into a panic:

> In terror I hid behind a piece of scenery, then I rushed on to the deserted stage and shouted to the pianist 'Play Tipperary'. He did, and I started to sing it to the fighting scrambling mass that was the audience. My actions had the desired effect, and some people began to applaud. Then Milton Rosmer returned and took up his lines with me, although I was not concerned with the lines he was speaking. We carried on until the other actors returned, and the show proceeded to a scanty auditorium.[35]

Zeppelin scares and darkened streets put some restraint on theatre-going, but attendances quickly reverted to pre-war numbers, especially in the provinces, partly due to the employment opportunities in the mammoth munitions industry resulting in increased disposable incomes (especially for women), and also because of the stationing of large numbers of troops. In 1915, Blackpool's theatres, for instance, experienced a prosperous war as attendances were boosted by thousands of British and colonial troops billeted in the town. There was more fluidity between hitherto separate variety and legitimate theatre audiences, too. The new social mix was looked down on by a *Bystander* columnist, who complained that: 'Up North there's such prosperity that at the theatres it's the best seats that are filled and the cheapest left empty, while the young women of the working classes who now "conduct" the trams and 'buses take stalls and boxes.'[36]

Another novel wartime theatre phenomenon was the soldier on ten days' leave having a night out, often taking spouses or sweethearts out to see a show. Gradually the theatre habit spread until every night in the week became a khaki night. With thousands of uniformed men floating around in London, it's no wonder that West End business boomed, especially revues with their flimsily dressed semi-erotic 'beauty chorus'. The usual class distinctions no longer applied and pre-war theatre rules of etiquette rapidly flew out of the window. As a *Times* journalist noted:

'Evening dress is no longer *de rigueur* in the West End stalls. It is the presence of khaki in the stalls that has done much to displace ordinary evening dress.'[37] To some wounded battle-hardened soldiers on leave, like the poet Robert Graves, the pleasure-seeking crowds seemed unreal:

> We could not understand the war-madness that ran wild everywhere, looking for a pseudo military outlet. The civilians talked a foreign language; and it was newspaper language.[38]

Within weeks of the Zeppelin attack in London, the Aldwych and Gaiety were back in business and the Lyceum redecorated in time for a pantomime season of *Robinson Crusoe*. The lethal reality of aerial bombardment might have shocked, but theatre was becoming a pseudo military safe haven; and pantomime was no exception. In pantomimes across the land, the second Christmas of war was a distinctly khaki Christmas. At the Lyceum, Nan C. Hearne played the title role in *Robinson Crusoe* dressed as a sailor boy singing 'Keep the Home Fires Burning', and ended the show dressed as a Red Cross warrior knight. The Aldwych featured Cressie Leonard as a khaki-clad Robin Hood ('Well there is nothing that you may not do in pantomime,' observed *The Times*).[39] In *Goody Two Shoes* at Bristol's Prince's Theatre, Sybil Arnsdale (Principal Boy) and Daisy Dormer (Principal Girl) encouraged the audience to join in with 'Pack Up Your Troubles' and 'Boys in Khaki'. At the Marlborough, in north London, the highlight of *Jack Horner* was Winifred Ward singing 'We All Did the Goose-step' while neatly attired as a Tommy in a kilt, backed by a chorus of boy scouts and highlanders.

Maybe khaki was a common enough sight in every theatre in Britain, but in London there was a special Yuletide poignancy about the new and disturbing phenomenon of row upon row of severely wounded or convalescing soldiers in their hospital blue uniforms invited to attend Christmas show dress rehearsals on Christmas Eve. Pantomimes were making a jolly spectacle of war – but on occasions like this it was impossible to shut out the depressing reality of war. At Drury Lane, wounded men arrived in the hundreds from hospitals around London to see the dress run of *Puss in Boots*. Tea was served in the interval in the saloon bar; those barely able to move had it brought to them by their more mobile comrades. At the Palladium, a *Daily Express* correspondent encountered a similar gut-wrenching scene – 'piercing in its pathos' – when, to calls of 'make way for the heroes' the wounded warriors filed though the foyer to climb aboard buses taking them back to their wards:

> There were crutches, arms in slings, bandages on heads and faces beyond all counting and God Save the King was thundered out with every man who could standing stiff at attention … shouts of 'bus number 12, those for bus number four' were the last sounds we heard as we left the theatre, and a surging crowd of khaki, grey and blue winding its way back to the hospitals was the last thing we saw.[40]

# 3

## 1916

### 'Smile! Dammit, smile!'

Saturday 1 January 1916. A poem by Jessie Pope in the morning's *Daily Express* ponders: 'What will this year, so new and small/Bring forth, I wonder, for us all?' On the war front, the New Year begins with Europe half in ruins and the battle lines extending from the Western Front to Mesopotamia. On the theatre industry front, 1916 will bring forth unforeseen challenges, including the imposition of a new Entertainments Tax. But in London on the first Saturday afternoon of the year 'Full House' signs are outside theatres packed with matinee crowds and messenger boys are on the streets whistling the new pantomime song, 'There's a Ship That's Bound for Blighty'. There's a sign that a war is on at Drury Lane, where both matinee and evening performances of *Puss in Boots* begin thirty minutes early in case of air raids. Most West End venues are taking similar precautions. Revues are falling over each other in a quest to stimulate national cheerfulness. In *Joyland* at the Hippodrome, singer Bertram Wallis fills the auditorium with a massive Union Jack to the tune of 'Our Own Dear Flag'; but the star is sketch comedian Harry Tate, who is so popular that his name is adopted by RAF fliers as a rhyming nickname for the new R.E.8. biplane. In what is still the season of good will, the Little Theatre at Charing Cross reopens its doors on this day as a YMCA soldiers' and sailors' social club with beds in the former dressing rooms, baths under the stage and billiards in the cloakroom. The location in John Street – near Charing Cross railway station – is handy for soldiers arriving from France. Over at Victoria Station, immediately opposite the Victoria Palace where 'The Kinema Cake Walk' is the jolly toe-tapping finale to *The Radium Girl*, there's no let-up in the streams of walking wounded. The atmosphere at the station is charged with more drama than usual when a squad of pressmen and theatre dignitaries rush forward to greet a lone figure from across the Channel – the world's most famous actress, Sarah Bernhardt.[1]

At the age of 72, the 'Divine Sarah' arrived London with a grim purpose – to perform a season of ferociously anti-German verse playlets at the Coliseum, followed by a lengthy provincial tour. Before making a grand exit along the station platform in a wheelchair (her right leg had been amputated following a gangrenous infection) Bernhardt made no bones about her loathing for Germans. Why were so many still allowed to live in London, she snapped at the pressmen: 'We have no Germans in France – even naturalised Germans are being sent away: you English are too generous, too confiding.'[2] Bernhard's two productions – *Les Cathédrals*, by the playwright and artist Eugene Morand, and *Du Théâtre au Champ d'Honneur* (*From the Stage to the Field of Honour*), written by an unknown French Army officer at the Front – both combined Hun hatred with fierce exhortations to endure the pain of fighting to the end, however much destruction it took. Performed in French with a company of actors from Paris, there was nothing quite like these incendiary quasi-religious pieces anywhere in British theatre, where revues, popular songs, musical comedies and plays continued to offer idealised images of war in various combinations of romantic escapism, patriotic cliché and sanitised versions of battlefield life. Bernhardt's blazing French oratory was in a different league of dramatic cliché altogether, attracting adoring audiences wherever she went. In London, the Coliseum was filled to its 2,300-seat

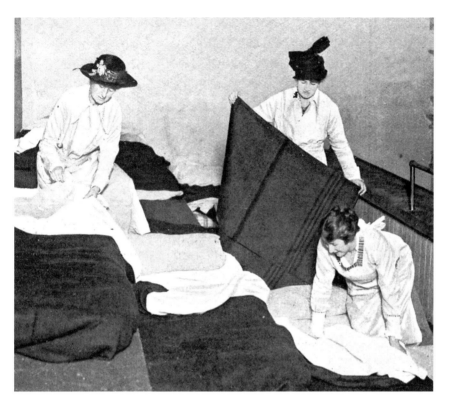

Volunteers making beds in the gallery of the Little Theatre, which was converted into a soldiers' club. (*The Sphere*/Author)

capacity for every performance. On 3 January, royalty attended the first matinee of *Les Cathédrals*, with its condemnation of German war crimes such as the murder of Edith Cavell, and climactic ending where the spire of Strasbourg Cathedral symbolically pierced the heart of a German eagle to a cry of '*aux armes!*' The image of fiendish Germany toppled couldn't have been more timely on a day that newspapers were full of the torpedoing without warning of the P&O liner *Persia* off Crete with the loss of 350 lives – 'Murder of the Innocents: Glad New Year for the Huns' was emblazoned across the *Daily Express* front page. Two weeks later, the elderly Bernhardt played a mortally wounded soldier boy in *Du Théâtre au*

*Champ d'Honneur*, a performance combining martyrdom with salvation hailed by one critic as 'packed full of the spirit of willing self-sacrifice and that white-hot flame of patriotism so splendidly characteristic of France at the moment'. An evening with the Divine Sarah wasn't entirely taken up with hawkish histrionics: it might seem peculiar to us, but nobody batted an eyelid when the accompanying variety bill included a troupe of trick cyclists, a short farce (*A Pair of Knickerbockers*) about a married feminist who insists on wearing male clothing, and a blistering turn from Britain's own cross-dressed soldier boy, Vesta Tilley.[3]

At the end of April, Bernhardt embarked for Paris after reprising *Du Théâtre au Champ d'Honneur* in London as part of what turned out to be one of British theatre's most successful single fund-raising events of the entire war – an all-star charity gala with the emphasis on what *The Times*

The white-hot flame of patriotism: Sarah Bernhardt in *Du Théâtre au Champ d'Honneur* at the Coliseum. (*The Illustrated War News*/Author)

described as the 'delicately feminine'. By February 1916, *The Era* calculated that money raised by theatrical and music hall performances for war charities exceeded £50,000. But on one single Friday afternoon (14 April) at the Theatre Royal Drury Lane, the equivalent of £250,000 today was raised as part of a YWCA national appeal to provide canteens and rest rooms for the nation's growing army of women munitions workers. The Queen and other members of the British and European royal families were present; Prime Minister Herbert Asquith and munitions minister David Lloyd George led a contingent of high-level politicians. In keeping with the fund-raising objective, dotted around the Coliseum auditorium selling programmes to the well-heeled audience, were women in tunics from munitions factories, who also provided a guard of honour for the royal party. Apart from Bernhardt's 'turn', the highlight of the afternoon was a kinematograph sequence depicting a day in the life of a munitions worker, though this being wartime there was no reference to the explosive dangers faced by 'munitionettes'. Other 'delicately feminine' items included a scene from Edward Knoblock's hit play *My Lady's Dress* and a short piece by J.M. Barrie about Shakespearean queens arguing over the nature of beauty, with a cast headed by glamorous musical comedy star Lily Elsie. The big pre-interval finale – a pageant entitled *Through Toil to Victory* – featured a replica munitions factory, an enactment of a Zeppelin raid and a battlefront scene, with real munitionettes onstage alongside actresses in symbolic poses – Viola Tree as 'Belgium', Lilian Braithwaite as 'Italy' and Hilda Trevelyan as 'She Who Crowns with Glory'.[4]

Promoting the event in the press, Bernhardt issued a rallying call: 'Men must fight, but this is not the time for women to weep,' she urged readers of *Everywoman's Weekly*. 'They must be strong in faith, active in war-work, inspiring as ever by their love and patriotism.'[5] By then, British women didn't need lecturing to fall in line. In March 1916 the Military Service Act was passed, imposing conscription, with some exemptions, on all single men aged between 18 and 41, followed by a second Conscription Act in May 1916 that extended conscription to married men. With so many men leaving to fight, women weren't only weeping when they left home or never returned; they weren't all Sister Suzys sewing shirts for soldiers. Hundreds of thousands of women of all classes and backgrounds kept home fires going by taking up former male-only jobs on farms, in factories, shops, offices and hospitals – and in the theatre industry.

Indeed, the success of the 'delicately feminine' Drury Lane munitions matinee was entirely due to the organising abilities of one woman – actress, theatre director and writer Olga Nethersole, who was renowned for her 'wicked women' roles and impassioned performances delivered very much in the Bernhardt style. In 1894, when she entered into management at the Royal Court Theatre at the age of 24, *Black and White* magazine hailed her as 'The English Bernhardt'.[6] But at the moment when the war offered women in the theatre heaven-sent opportunities to show they were perfectly capable of carrying out men's jobs, Nethersole joined the British Red Cross, serving for the duration on the nursing staff of Hampstead Military Hospital as a Voluntary Aid Detachment member. In 1917, she established the People's League of Health, campaigning to raise national health standards, for which she was created a Commander of the British Empire in 1936.[7]

In 1916, conscription arrived on the statute book just when show business was experiencing an unforeseen boom. Men between the age of 18 and 41 could be withdrawn from their workplace at any time, although some rare exemptions were made for those employed in work of 'national importance', the medically unfit and approved conscientious objectors. With more than 2,000 members of the theatre profession already in the services, the issue now was how to keep shows on the road and profits up. One lesson that theatre managements had learned was that the provision of live entertainment was not only psychologically vital for the national effort, but that the war economy had actually given a boost to the industry's commercial sustainability.

Company reports published in March 1916 made excellent reading for shareholders of the important London and provincial syndicates and smaller touring circuits. A sure sign of business confidence occurred

Women filled former male-only backstage jobs, like this stage door keeper. (Topfoto/ArenaPAL; www.arenapal.com)

in November 1916 when a brand-new West End theatre opened, the St Martin's, with revue maestro Charles B. Cochran as lessee. As an editorial in *The Era* explained, never were theatres more popular, providing 'abundant evidence that the favourable industrial conditions of the country, greatly benefited by the absence of unemployment and by the lavish expenditure of public money, have prompted very large expenditure by the masses of wage-earners on their favourite forms of entertainment'.[8] Surprising perhaps, when bodies were piling up and graves getting deeper by the day in France. But then this was also a time when looking cheerful and putting on a smiling face in public was almost a national duty – even if the jaws of hell were gaping somewhere at the back of most minds. London's wartime West End theatre not only became lucrative, but a place where pleasure-making and untold internal horrors were able to co-exist. The writer and pacifist Caroline Playne observed the contradiction in May 1916:

> A bright day, London crowded with well-dressed, if not exactly gaily dressed, people… the theatres, music halls and picture palaces were filling up… all was as usual on a May day in London. Only the background was grim, for one's eye caught posters having 'The Charnel House of Verdun' as the prominent headline that afternoon.[9]

At first compulsory service wiped the smiles off the faces of theatre managements, worried about the loss of backstage personnel, front of house staff and younger actors. In the end, despite an argument that the entire profession ought to be exempted from conscription because it employed skilled labour and 'lightened the burden of war-time life', the measure was accepted, although the critic Henry Belcham, writing in *The Era Annual*, reckoned that while men 'from the highest class companies of the West End to the humble caravan of the showmen joined up gladly', their loss was severely felt: 'The depletion of stage staff has crippled production, but even more serious has been the abstraction of a large number of the rank and file of the profession from revues and theatres.' By the end of May, twenty-five members of staff at Stoll's Manchester Hippodrome had been called up; others were about to go, their places taken by older men. At the nearby King's Theatre, part of the northern Broadhead syndicate, all but three of the stage staff were absent and women took over 'light duties'. The manager of the Lyceum Theatre, Ipswich, claimed that his entire backstage and front-of-house staff were now women ('even to a manager') and only older actors were appearing onstage. By then, *The Era* had already noted that it was now 'quite an ordinary experience to have on the stage Charles Surfaces and Captain Absolutes and Young Marlows of 45 to 50 years of age'.[10] Concerned about those actors left behind looking 'flat and insipid' onstage, the paper came up with a novel suggestion – that women should step into the breach and take on the male roles:

> At the present juncture, a great many male occupations are undertaken by women. Why should not there spring up a special class of actresses impersonating men in plays? Not long before the war, the Suffragettes were claiming equality with Man in many ways, and they had many supporters amongst actresses, and have now. From them we hope some of the male impersonators whom we speculate upon will spring.[11]

Gender-swapping never took off, although one large-scale management exploited the curiosity value of an 'all-women' production. Fred Karno, the comedy genius who encouraged Charlie Chaplin's early comic potential, sent out a touring revue entitled *All Ladies*, later changed to *All Women*. At one point, the show had a cast of eight principals, including forces' sweetheart Gertie Gitana (of 'Nellie Dean' fame), a forty-strong female chorus and a stage management run by women. At each theatre, Emmie Thomas conducted pit orchestras made up of local musicians; but the scriptwriters were all men.

In the variety sector, an additional fear was the possible invasion of American artists hoping to fill the gaps left by British performers. In May, just before the Military Services Act was extended to include

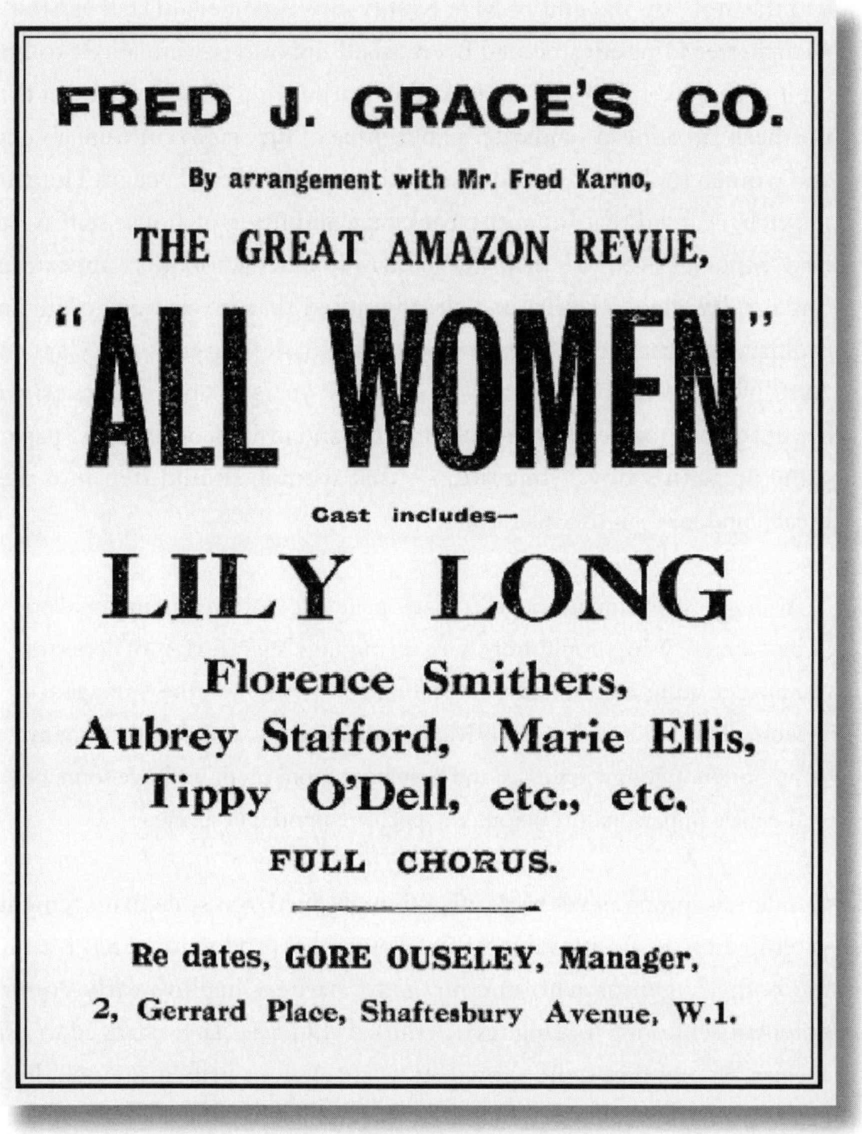


Fred Karno's touring all-women revue. (*The Era*)

married men, the Variety Artistes' Federation even cabled their American counterpart to warn their performers not to accept British engagements, otherwise they would 'adopt all possible means to prevent foreign artists playing'. This was followed up by an equally stern statement sent to British managements:

> British performers feel it will outrage all canons of loyalty and patriotism and engender a bitter feeling of injustice if foreigners are imported for the specific purpose of filling the places of those called upon to sacrifice their interests, and maybe their lives, for the welfare of those who remain behind whilst there are others of their own countrymen able and willing to step into the breach for the time being.[12]

The American takeover didn't happen, but new conscription rules meant tremors backstage whenever the police scoured theatres for suspected draft dodgers. In September 1916, during a Saturday night police raid at Edmonton Empire, actor Joseph Essangay was arrested in the middle of playing the romantic lead in *Her Great Love*. He subsequently told the local tribunal that his parents were Mexican, he was over-age, for the past three years had been touring Ireland and was not registered as he had left England before the war. The chairman ruled that his story was unprovable and Essangay was handed over to the military authorities.[13] During operations in Royal Victoria Park, Bath, police picked up Tom Percival Brightener, the proprietor of an al fresco pierrot show, who claimed he was Irish. He was remanded to await an escort. Police raids didn't always go as planned. When two detectives arrived at an Edinburgh stage door demanding to know why a smart 'young single fellow' was in the show, it turned out they'd been keeping an eye on male impersonator Teddie Le Roy. Even then her husband, Ted Le Roy, had to produce their marriage certificate; and Teddie was made to remove her stage wig to prove her femininity. Some exemptions were upheld. A tour manager appealing to the Dewsbury tribunal argued that he was responsible for three companies employing more than 160 people and was therefore indispensable. Asked if he thought his work was of national importance, he replied: 'If there were no amusements people would have nowhere to go.' He was granted three months' grace.[14] Much later, in 1918, when the age limit was raised to 51, high-earning comedian Harry Tate, aged 46, was declared exempt from service by Wandsworth Tribunal, the thinking being that Tate was already a member of the Motor Transport Volunteers, and if he joined up the country would lose a fortune each year in super-income tax.

The idea of raising money for the exchequer through a tax on entertainment was not new: it was usually dismissed because the small revenue was thought to be hardly worth the expense of collecting it. But when on 4 April 1916, as part of his war budget, Chancellor Reginald McKenna announced a graduated tax to be levied on all forms of public entertainment, including theatres and cinemas, some estimates suggested that the tax on theatre admissions in London and its suburbs alone could bring in a weekly revenue of £10,000. Prophesying financial disaster was the instant management default position whenever wartime emergency legislation came along. This year, if it wasn't worries about the effect on profits of daylight saving, or having to close theatres at 10.30 p.m., it was the fear of losing out on bar takings when the Early Closing Order banned the sale of confectionary and tobacco in theatres after 8 p.m.. Anxieties about the financial impact of an Entertainments Tax were, therefore, initially at a high pitch. Is the paying public prepared to pay a halfpenny or a shilling extra to see a show? How will the tax be gathered? Who picks up the admin costs involved in collection and filling in returns? B. W. Findon, the veteran editor of the monthly *Play Pictorial* magazine, was in no doubt: the idea was simply unfair: 'It does seem a little incongruous that one should be penalised for entering a theatre while you can buy the most expensive luxuries at the Army and Navy Stores without a stamp being added to your ticket of membership.'[15]

Several high-level deputations of West End and provincial managerial associations met with tax officials: one touring manager, Edward Compton, issued a dire warning that the tax 'would probably prove a death-blow to a large number of small managers'. But Customs and

Excise was not for turning. When the Act came into force on 15 May 1916, the tax was added to the normal ticket price (typically, threepence on a shilling ticket) and local reporters from *The Stage* found the scheme 'working throughout the land'. In London, business was 'quite as good as before the tax came into operation'. It was a similar story of packed houses and very little grumbling elsewhere. Charles Bush, manager of the Queen's Theatre, Leeds, was so pleased with the way things went at the box office that prior to the Monday matinee of *You're Pulling My Leg* he stood before the curtain and thanked the audience for 'helping to make the collection of the tax so easy'. However, not everyone was onside. J.P. Mullholland of Wimbledon Theatre and the King's Theatre Hammersmith printed a programme note pointing out that managers had effectively become unpaid tax-gatherers:

> They must be penalised for continuing to exist. The form and directions supplied by the Government may be viewed at the box office. As examples of ignorance, red tape, and incapacity they are well worth examination.

But J.F. Elliston, controller of several theatres in the Bolton area, told *The Stage* that there were no complaints from his patrons because he prepared them by publishing an advance statement in his programmes:

> Grasp the idea that theatre is not quite a luxury. It is a great industry employing directly and indirectly millions of workers.
> Healthy and reasonable recreation is as essential as food. The rate we live at – the high speed that workers have to work – makes relaxation an absolute necessity.
> As Patriots and Britishers, treat this Tax as you do all others, and console yourselves that the need is *pressing*, the cause is *just*, and the sacrifice *small*.[16]

Initially an emergency measure, the Entertainments Tax provided a large enough return to remain on the statute book until 1960. But wartime proceeds from taxing entertainment were complemented by the seemingly boundless charitable efforts of the entertainment industry. From organising big gala occasions to individual generosity, without any prompting theatre launched into what Bernard Shaw called 'the passionate penny collecting of the Flag Days'.[17] It became virtually impossible to buy a theatre ticket without stumping up a bit extra for one of the money-raising stunts held night after night in every theatre in the land. By early 1916, show business was playing an integral part in the huge national welfare effort, supporting organisations such as the YMCA, Red Cross, Belgian Relief Fund the Blind Heroes Fund, Actors' Benevolent Fund, the Variety Artistes' Benevolent Fund and numerous local charities. As B. W. Findon, of *Play Pictorial*, observed: 'Here, there and everywhere, individual artists and managers have been unsparing in their efforts to accomplish some good towards the common end.'[18]

By early 1916, the Actors' Benevolent Fund had not only received record amounts from special performances and organisations such as the Playgoers' Club, but had handed out more than £6,000 to relieve hardship in the profession. One fund-raising drive exemplifies the determination of individuals to join the rush to help. Dora Gregory, appearing in *Kultur at Home* at the Strand Theatre, an anti-German drama about an Englishwoman marrying a Prussian officer who turns into a military despot, started her own tobacco fund after three Tommies sent her a cheeky begging letter when they came across a scrap of newspaper blowing around in their trench. They wrote:

> Picking it up to read, as it is our only means of getting news of the outside world, we were a little dismayed to find that it only contained a bit of theatrical news, chiefly concerning the play called Kultur at Home. We were just going to throw it over to the Germans when a bright idea crossed us. Why, here we are roughing it out here and having a bit of fun with baby-killers, and we are short of our mainstay – tobacco, and as we don't get much supply we thought by sending to you and your fellow-chums in your play we might be able to find someone who would like to help us on with our smoke.[19]

MISS JOSE COLLINS AND MR. LAURI DE FRECE
in "THE MAID OF THE MOUNTAINS," at Daly's Theatre, London.

Theatre stars, such as Jose Collins and Lauri de Frece of *The Maid of the Mountains* and Nelson Keys, sold signed postcards to raise cash for *The Performer* magazine's Tobacco Fund, (Author)

Gregory immediately set to work, raising money from the company and then publicising her fund in *The Stage*. Another solo initiative was the Wounded Soldiers' Matinee Tea Fund established by *Play Pictorial's* B.W. Findon. Each week until 1918, Findon ferried a party of wounded soldiers from the Military Hospital in Endell Street, Covent Garden, to a West End matinee, followed by high tea at the Embankment Gardens Tearooms, and gave out cigarettes and free evening newspapers before returning them back to the wards. By the end of 1916, when London hospitals were becoming seriously overcrowded, Findon had drummed up enough cash from his readers to send more than 1,000 wounded soldiers on show-and-tea outings. A monthly appeal in the magazine was usually matched by an account of the impact the matinees had on the men: 'Two hours and a half in a London theatre is a fine tonic. If you could be with me as they say "good-night" you would not grudge your "bit".' The point was picked up by a Lieutenant White, who sent Findon a guinea for the fund:

> If a few of our philanthropists at home had seen some of the sights, smelt the stink shells, and had some of their eyes water with tear shells, they too would send along a few sixpences. From what I know of Tommy, he prefers a little outing like you are giving to any tea party in Berkeley Square with flunkies hanging around, and no old aunties to ask him if it hurt when he was hit.[20]

Wednesday, 12 July 1916 was a 'Forget-me-not Day' – one of a myriad of street collection days. This time though, members of the Music Hall Ladies' Guild collected on behalf of a new national cause with a theatrical connection – the War Seal Foundation. In May, the Foundation received permission to build a block of seventy-two self-contained flats for permanently disabled soldiers and their families on a site in Fulham Road, west London, next to Chelsea Football Club and directly opposite the new Lord Roberts Memorial Workshop, providing practical training for disabled ex-servicemen. The War Seal Mansions project aimed to fulfil

A common sight by 1916; wounded soldiers arriving for a matinee outside the Theatre Royal and Opera House, Stockport (Author)

another growing need and was the brainchild of the philanthropically minded impresario Oswald Stoll, who donated the land and then set about raising funds to build the flats. Most of the cash came through the sale of small diamond-shaped War Seals at a halfpenny each; and Stoll's idea of using them for sealing letters or sticking on postcards soon caught on. Seals could be purchased at all Stoll theatres, and were also available at stores such as Boots and Selfridges (both Sir Jesse Boot and Gordon Selfridge were on the governing board, as was the Prime Minister's wife, Margot Asquith). *As The Stage* noted when fund-raising got under way, 'the beauty of the scheme is that all can help'. Individual War Seal sellers included singer Julien Henry, who sold £3,000-worth during a three-week run at the Coliseum before leaving to join his regiment – although he was assisted by a team of actresses who did a roaring trade by selling four kisses with each Seal for a sovereign. Comedy duo Mooney and

Holbein donated their entire week's salary at the Shepherd's Bush Empire, where a concert on 26 March raised another £400, which made this Stoll-owned theatre the first place of entertainment to endow a flat. Stars who paid for dedicated flats included Gertie Gitana and Vesta Tilley.[21]

Stoll's efforts earned him a knighthood in 1919 for 'valuable work for many charities', though his biographer, Felix Barker, thought that he would have far preferred to have been cited for 'services to the variety theatre'.[22] Throughout the war years Stoll opened up the Coliseum to a succession of mammoth midweek and Sunday evening charity events, many of them hosted by George Robey. A typical gala took place on 9 June 1916, when Queen Mary, Patron of the British Red Cross Society, attended in aid of the Star and Garter home in Richmond for severely disabled ex-servicemen, which opened in January 1916 but had reached capacity by June and needed to expand. In March, another royal

If you are grateful to the soldiers & sailors who are doing so much, will you support

## THE WAR SEAL FOUNDATION

by purchasing and using WAR SEALS?

THE ENTIRE PROCEEDS RESULTING FROM THE SALE OF WAR SEALS

are being devoted to the erection of dwellings wherein the disabled service man can live upon his pension with his wife and family, with his medical needs provided for on the spot, without any appeal to charity.

Advertisement for Oswald Stoll's War Seals scheme. (Stoll)

gala matinee in support of Lena Ashwell's YMCA-funded Concerts at the Front raised the princely sum of £700. A surprise item created a sensation – the first screening of *The Real Thing at Last*, a silent film comedy inspired by news of an American 'picture play' of *Macbeth*, directed by D.W. Griffith. Barrie's thirty-minute spoof pitched *Macbeth* as performed by British actors against the play as treated by Hollywood and. It starred Edmund Gwenn, who worked on the film while on leave from the Royal Army Service Corps, where he had reached the rank of captain, and who was destined for a post-war career in Hollywood.

*The Real Thing at Last* was timely because it parodied Hollywood-ised Shakespeare at the precise moment when thoroughly British images of the playwright, who died 300 years before the battle of the Somme, were appropriated to generate new heights of nationalistic fervour during a national four-day Shakespeare Tercentenary Celebration. The Stratford-upon-Avon part of the festival included keynote productions by the Frank Benson company at the Memorial Theatre (Benson had been presenting annual summer Shakespeare seasons there for twenty years), a Shakespeare Pageant and church sermons on 'Shakespeare Sunday' praising the national poet as a beacon of English-speaking civilisation. London had a three-week, Martin Harvey-led season at His Majesty's Theatre, with proceeds going to the Red Cross Fund, and there were productions at the Old Vic. Academics delivered stern lectures on Germany's 'misappropriation' of Shakespeare as an equal to Goethe and Schiller, and a wooden mock-Tudor style YMCA 'Shakespeare Hut' for Anzac servicemen on leave was built on a street corner site in Bloomsbury. 'Shakespeare Day', 3 May, was observed in schools and accompanied by a special booklet, *Notes on Shakespeare the Patriot*, written by Israel Gollancz, Secretary of the Tercentenary organising committee, who also edited a weighty *Book of Homage to Shakespeare* with contributions from 160 literary and theatrical 'homagers' from across the British Empire and allied countries.

At least for a few days, Shakespeare could be invoked as the ultimate patriot–soldier, or mobilised as the nation's war poet. Quoting from

Shakespeare the patriot: characters in *Henry V* acted by the Frank Benson company at Stratford-upon-Avon. (*The Sphere*/Author)

*King John* ('This England never did, nor never shall/Lie at the feet of a conqueror'), Gollancz urged patriotic schoolchildren to learn the lessons Shakespeare had left behind through his 'gentle grace and modesty and his ability to reach out to everyone'.[23] Writing in *The Sphere*, Shakespeare scholar Sir Sydney Lee took up the cause, urging the entire nation to don the playwright's 'intellectual armour' as a 'munition of war' and one of the 'spurs to present action by land, sea, and air'.[24] A mythical warrior Shakespeare was even employed to encourage the wavering United States to join the Allies. While performing in New York, Beerbohm Tree made patriotic speeches using Shakespeare to swing American opinion. When the American Ambassador to Britain, Walter Hines Page, who was involved in planning the tercentenary events, invited the President of Harvard to represent his country at the celebrations, he wrote:

> The most important duty that now lies on every English-speaking man is to make sure of an active sympathy between the peoples of the United States and the British Empire; for the peace of the world and the maintenance and progress of civilization depend on this sympathy and there is no other basis of hope.[25]

On 4 May, a *Shakespeare Tercentenary Commemoration Performance* at Drury Lane, in the presence of the King and Queen, made national news when the King knighted Frank Benson behind the royal box during the interval – the actor was still wearing his Julius Caesar costume and the theatre manager had to send out for a prop sword. But the real weaponry of war was never far away. In sleepy Stratford, centenary productions at the Memorial Theatre were thrown into crisis when members of Benson's company were suddenly called to the colours. The plays had to be recast. When the newly knighted Sir Frank and Lady Benson arrived in triumph at Stratford, *The Era* reported how they drove through crowd-lined streets and past the hospital, 'where wounded heroes on blue and khaki, so often the guests of the Benson's at the theatre, were gathered to add their tribute to the general acclamation'.[26] As a huge 'Shakespeare Sunday' procession streamed through Stratford to Holy Trinity Church, the organ pealed out the anthems of the Allies; then Benson delivered his 'Once more unto the breach' speech, having already given an Agincourt spin on the relevance of 'our national poet to war and peace' during an address to a British Empire Shakespeare Society gathering in London. There would never have been a war at all, Benson argued, if Europe had properly understood Shakespeare 'and all he had to say about the brotherhood of man ... but they have the words "I mock at death", and that is what our khaki knights are so splendidly doing across the water'. Meanwhile, close to the killing fields of France and not far from the historic ones at Agincourt, a less grandiose tercentenary celebration took place in the 'Kinema Hut' at the No. 1 Camp near Calais, where Major L.M. Shaw-Page, Captain G.T. Heath, Lieutenant W.J.F. Anderson Raby and other 'khaki knights' performed scenes from *Twelfth Night* and *Henry V* – wigs, make-up and costumes courtesy of London costumier Willy Clarkson.[27]

There were no more Benson seasons at the Memorial Theatre after the 1916 festivities. By now in his late 50s, Sir Frank went to the Front: first with his wife's canteen for soldiers, then as an ambulance driver collecting the wounded in the firing line. 'So many actors have thrown up everything and gone to the front that we felt that we ought to do what we could,' he told a London reporter. 'After talking Shakespeare for so many years, I think that one ought to "do Shakespeare" if the chance offers.'[28] Two months later, the Bensons' son Eric, the youngest lieutenant colonel in the Army, was awarded the Military Cross and was about to become a brigadier general when he was killed. Today, in the Swan Building at the Royal Shakespeare Theatre at Stratford, Eric's image forms part of a memorial stained-glass window commemorating ten of Benson's actor 'khaki knights' who died in battle.

Ironically, the Tercentenary coming together of exalted patriotism, theatrical sentimentalism and cultural appropriation was never reflected in a resurgence of audience interest in Shakespeare, a phenomenon noticed by the theatre critic E.A. Baughan, who thought that the flurry of productions did not point to 'any great love of Shakespeare, although one would have thought his plays were just the kind of serious drama audiences would like in war time'.[29] Apart from the Tree, Benson and Martin Harvey seasons, productions at the Old Vic and the efforts of a few provincial repertory companies, plays by the 'soldier–poet' were notoriously bad box office. Generally, British audiences were used to seeing excerpts from Shakespeare cut down to about half an hour performed by revered actors, often as part of a variety bill. In 1916, Stoll's Coliseum set a rather faded gold standard for these illustrious star turns. At the age of 58, Mary Anderson appeared in the balcony scene from *Romeo and Juliet,* reprising the role of Juliet she had first played at the age of 16. The now 70-year-old Ellen Terry also came out of retirement to appear in scenes from *The Merry Wives of Windsor*. She then took Portia from *The Merchant of Venice* on a variety tour, carrying on regardless during a Zeppelin raid when the bombs seemed to fall in time with each line of her keynote speech, 'The quality of mercy is not strained/ It droppeth as the gentle rain from heaven.' Her daughter recalled how the sound of the audience cheering after each line 'made the noise of the infernal overhead machines inaudible'.[30]

In reality, laughter and song rallied the nation, not Shakespearean verse. Laughing in a theatre could get you through whatever turmoil you might be experiencing in your personal life, even if a show lasted only two hours and you had to negotiate charity collection boxes, overtly patriotic interval music, actors onstage looking older than they used to be, and when the latest war news was being flashed on to a screen and the posters outside alerted you of the danger of Zeppelin raids. As the journalist Michael MacDonagh noted in his diary: 'Even in wartime with all its gloom hilarity will keep breaking in. No situation is ever so bad that it might not be much worse.'[31] Most theatre managements had come to the same conclusion: that purveyors of good-humoured light entertainment were the ones who sold seats, which led Bernard Shaw to complain that the war 'completely upset the economic conditions which formerly enabled serious drama to pay its way in London'. E.A. Baughan, writing in the *Stage Yearbook*, thought that in 1916, 'comedy, farce, revues, and plays of spectacle are the only dramatic fare play-goers require … They do not want to be reminded of the war, and resent any talk of heroism.' There was, he went on, nothing shameful in thinking that:

> out there at the front our men are facing death and worse than death itself while here at home we laugh and smile … we, no less than the fighting men, have our sorrows and our troubles. 'Smile! Dammit, smile!', an inscription on a dug-out in France, is the best antidote to the poison of war.[32]

Enough of war plays: cartoon by Norman Morrow. (Illustrated London News Ltd/Mary Evans)

Happiness onstage: *The Bing Boys are Here*, starring Alfred Lester, Violet Lorraine and George Robey, introduced 'If You Were the Only Girl In the World' – a wartime favourite. (Author)

Mabel Koopman, of *The Era*, who became the first 'lady critic' to be admitted to the Critics' Circle in 1916, had her finger on the pulse too: 'With the thoughts of the entire nation focused on the gigantic struggle between Slavery and Freedom, is it to be wondered at that in moments of relaxation the sanest turn naturally to plays that demand little thought and less feeling?'[33]

So it's no coincidence that 1916, the year of the nightmare of the Somme offensive, also turned out to be the year of light revues such as *We're All in it*, *High Jinks* and *The Happy Day*, and also the moment when two of the most undemanding shows of the war blossomed into two of the most popular. *The Bing Boys are Here* and *Chu Chin Chow* caught the escapist zeitgeist, their happiness content attracting crowds like musical magnets. Another smile generator was to follow: *The Maid of the Mountains* premiered at His Majesty's Theatre in February 1917, after previews at the Prince's Theatre in Manchester in December 1916. But from August 1916, onwards *The Bing Boys* and *Chu Chin Chow* were *the* must-see shows, playing to full houses in the West End – at the same time as the seventy-five-minute War Office film *The Battle of the Somme* was being screened at the Scala Theatre and subsequently at more than thirty London cinemas simultaneously. Cinemas were screening darkness and destruction: theatres were all bright lights, sweet music and smiling togetherness.

Subtitled 'A Picture of London Life in a Prologue and Six Panels', *The Bing Boys* starred George Robey in his first full-length musical revue, comedy actor Alfred Lester and Violette Lorraine. The production was an instant success, running for twelve months to crowded houses with six matinees a week. It was the first of a series of *Bing Boys* revues that played at the Alhambra until well beyond the Armistice, including *The Bing Boys on Broadway* and *The Bing Girls are Here*. The songs soon spilled over from the Leicester Square venue to the Front, thanks to recordings made for the Columbia label, including 'Let the Great Big World Keep Turning' and a risqué Robey monologue hinting at marital infidelity, 'I stopped, I

**IF YOU WERE THE ONLY GIRL IN THE WORLD (1).**

Sometimes when I feel bad and things look blue,
I wish a girl I had—say one like you;
Someone within my heart to build her throne,
Someone who'd never part, to call my own.
I'll try a love to teach, dear, fond and true,
I sigh a world to reach, dear, just made for me and you.

BAMFORTH COPYRIGHT                    WORDS BY PERMISSION OF B FELDMAN & CO

From stage to postcards: The Bing Boys' hit song soon spilled over into popular culture. (Bamforth)

looked, and I listened', which was banned when the touring production reached Birmingham. Not surprisingly, the show-stopping Robey-Lorraine love duet, 'If You Were the Only Girl in the World', became a forces favourite. Robey reckoned the loveliest thing of all, though, was not the songs or the show, but the wartime 'togetherness' between actors and audiences inside the Alhambra – how everyone 'carried on while air-raids were banging and booming overhead, and how the audience sat through them enjoying it as if the only sound outside was the twittering of the sparrows in Leicester Square.'[34] Even so, according to Michael MacDonagh's London diary, there was a tendency to stay in behind well-curtained windows during a full moon when Zeppelins raids were more likely:

> When the moon is out Zeppelins stay in, and we can go to the theatre with an easy mind. Places of entertainment have begun, in fact, to advertise 'moony nights' as holiday resorts do 'sunny days'. 'Come and see the *Bing Boys*: it is a full moon to-night so you need not fear the "Bang Boys".' The streets were thronged with carefree crowds 'mooning' themselves.[35]

Meanwhile, as men lay dead or wounded on moonlit battle zones and 'Somme' had become a byword for catastrophe, *Chu Chin Chow*, opening on 31 August – just days after the press reported mass casualties of more than 6,000 men over one weekend – offered its own exotic brand of togetherness with a rich mix of Arabian Nights, revue and pantomime. Produced, written and directed by Oscar Asche, who also played the lead role, this 'musical tale of the East' in thirteen scenes hoped to follow the success of *Kismet* in 1911 but more than surpassed it, running at Beerbohm Tree's His Majesty's for five years, effectively killing off Tree's annual Shakespeare seasons. Lavish sets and a parade of fashions made audiences gasp; chorus girls in revealing costumes attracted soldiers on leave. An *Observer* reviewer praised the dresses, or lack of them.[36]

The slave market scene in *Chu Chin Chow*, which opened at His Majesty's Theatre in 1916 and ran for five years. The show was particularly popular with soldiers on leave due to the scantily clad slave girls in the cast. (Illustrated London News Ltd/Mary Evans)

But even in *Chu Chin Chow*-land there was no escaping the trials of wartime. Because of the severe shortage of male backstage staff, the scheduled Wednesday afternoon dress rehearsal had to be moved to the evening when more casual labour was available; and patrons couldn't ignore air raid warning instructions plastered all over the foyer either, although the show's programme offered some reassurance to anyone who didn't want to rush home whenever there was a suspicious bang outside and whispers of 'Zepp!' flew around the auditorium:

> The tiers and main portion of the ceiling of the Theatre being constructed
> of steel and concrete, danger from falling shrapnel is remote, but those
> who desire more shelter that the Auditorium affords would find it in the
> Corridors, Bars, Staircases etc.[37]

At the end of the year, more exotica was on show in *Three Cheers!*, a new revue at the Shaftesbury Theatre with a flimsy plot featuring a spectacular Persian palace scene and an alluring 'Queen of Love' wearing an even flimsier costume. Apart from the 'beauty chorus', the big draw was Scottish comedian Harry Lauder, who stormed the audience with a rousing rendition of the self-penned 'The Laddies Who've Fought and Won' – a song heralding certain victory, even during the shocking aftermath of the Somme. Lauder remembered *Three Cheers!* as 'one of the gay shows that London liked because it gave some relief from the war and made the Zeppelin raids that the Huns were beginning to make so often now a little easier to bear.' He played Angus McAngus, who volunteers to fight and remains faithful to the lassie he leaves behind, but Lauder saw his main role as a cheerleader for the survivors of the mud, grime and horror who came to see the show:

> We owed them all we could give them. A man who has two days' leave in London does not want to see a serious play or a problem drama, as a rule. He wants something light, with lots of pretty girls and jolly tunes and people to make him laugh.

In the show, Lauder generated plenty of what *The Times* called 'boundless enthusiasm' when he sang about fighting 'till victory's won', after which 'all the lassies will be loving all the laddies' in an electrifying finale during which his Scottish Highlander character marched onstage accompanied by a squad of real Scots Guards, sanctioned to appear by the War Office. After the war, Lauder remembered night after night at the Shaftesbury being full of cheering officers and men, but how at the end of 1916 his own mood changed overnight. On New Year's Eve, a Sunday, he spent all day thinking about his own laddie fighting in France – Captain John Lauder of the First 8th Argyll and Sutherland Highlanders – and his plans for the young man's wedding in January: 'I did not feel right ... whatever the reason, I was depressed and blue, and I could not enter into the festive spirit that folk were trying to keep alive despite the war.'[38] Next morning, after a sleepless night at his Russell Square hotel, there was a hammering at the door. A porter delivered a telegram. It read: 'Captain John Lauder killed in action. Official. War Office.'

# 4

## 1917

### Old Bill wears his medals

Thursday, 4 January 1917. The morning papers feature an upbeat New Year message from Field Marshal Douglas Haig addressed to Ben Tillett, leader of the National Transport Workers' Federation. It ends: 'The workers have done splendidly in the past; we look for even greater efforts in the future. If the men and women workers at home and the troops in the trenches pull together, the triumph of our cause is certain.' In *The Times* there's also a downbeat message: today's Roll of Honour lists more than 2,000 British troops who pulled together in battle but were killed, wounded, missing or shell-shocked. Later this evening, in London, 2,000 men and women, many in uniform, are seated in the Shaftesbury Theatre eagerly anticipating Harry Lauder's return to *Three Cheers!* after a three-day closure following the death of his son John.[1]

On New Year's Day, once the bad news had sunk in that John was another Roll of Honour casualty, Lauder immediately returned home to Scotland, agonising over whether to withdraw from *Three Cheers!* altogether: 'Go out before an audience and seek to make it laugh? Sing my songs when my heart was broken?' On the other hand, fans implored him to return and the jobs of performers and staff at the Shaftesbury were at stake if he didn't go back. Then he remembered John's reported last words to his men – 'Carry on!' So, on this Thursday night, pale under his stage make-up, the still-grieving star stepped from the wings for his first number in the show, 'I Love My Jean', but his voice vanished in an explosion of cheering and shouts of 'Bravo, Harry!'. Grown men and women were in tears: many had probably also lost sons. Buoyed by the atmosphere of togetherness in adversity, Lauder got through the rest of the show – until the finale, when the audience sensed him faltering over the words in 'The Laddies Who Fought and Won': 'When we all gather round the old fireside, and the fond mother kisses her son …'. Lauder wrote about the song in a war memoir, published in 1918: 'Were they not cruel words for me to have to sing? My son was gone – he would never come back with the laddies who had fought and won!' A *Times* reporter was in no doubt that Lauder seemed to transcend his own stagecraft, turning shared grief into a collective experience of wartime loss:

> There has been no patriotic singing like this since the war began. He meant it so intensely, he threw into it so much genuine passion, that he appeared, not as a mere entertainer, but as the very voice of all those who have no voice of their own, while at the command of their deepest feelings they are labouring, enduring, suffering.[2]

Once *Three Cheers!* ended its run, Lauder 'carried on' at a phenomenal pace, first by entertaining in France. Too old to enlist at 47 and told that he would serve the nation better by performing, he gained official War Office support to travel right up to the battle lines where the troops were in the thick of it. When he embarked from Folkestone on 7 June, he was accompanied by James Hogge MP, a well-known known champion of Army and Navy pensions, and the Reverend George Adam, who gave short morale-boosting talks about the progress of the war. Wearing trench helmets, the trio dubbed 'The Reverend Harry Lauder, MP Tour' took a

Harry Lauder in *Three Cheers!* (Author)

custom-built piano, and a car-load of cigarettes to give away, and during two months roaming in the war-ravaged countryside around Arras, Bapaume, Péronne and Vimy Ridge, Lauder performed thirty minutes of show business camaraderie to small groups of men squatting at the roadside or in front of huge gatherings, often giving seven shows a day, frequently with live shellfire accompaniment. Once he sang 'Roamin' in the Gloamin'' for a crowd of Canadians seated in an amphitheatre created from a colossal shell crater. A member of a Highland regiment described being in a huge audience of kilted soldiers when Lauder had them all 'in fits of laughter for nearly an hour'.[3] This entertainer was not simply carrying on: he was on a mission. Back in Blighty, Lauder set about raising money for 'giving maimed Scots soldiers a fresh start in life', known officially as The Harry Lauder Million Pound Fund for Maimed Men, Scottish Soldiers and Sailors. His propagandising skills were then put to use on a government-backed tour of the United States and Canada to promote solidarity with British war aims, for which he wrote another rousing song – 'From the North and the South and the East and the West' – as an anthem for American troops.[4]

Of all Lauder's many self-penned songs, his everlasting legacy is the resolve-strengthening number he was inspired to compose immediately after his son's death. Over the decades, the original gritty grimness of 'Keep Right on to the End of the Road' has changed to mean different things at different times. In the 'carry on' atmosphere of early 1917, however, this was the right song with the right sentiment, arriving at precisely the moment when workers were being urged to make 'greater efforts in the future', with a lyric skilfully designed for participation by live theatre audiences who really were becoming, 'tired and weary', as the song goes, even if they didn't show it in public. By then, numerous music hall and revue numbers were promoting a similar trudge onwards theme; though who now can hum 'Slog on, Slog on, for 1917', or the Florrie Forde number 'We Must Keep on Keeping on'. In early 1917, still immersed in grief, Lauder summoned up all those qualities that made him a stage star to express in personality and performance a national mood of grim endurance and a need to keep on pulling together up the 'long steep hill'. In reality, there was no 'land of joy' in view and the triumph of the cause was far from certain; but this was gutsy stuff avoiding cock-a-hoop patriotism and, in some mysterious 'music hall' way, became part of life.

Glimpses of an emerging, more sombre national mood could even be detected in this year's pantomimes. According to a Christmas show survey in *The Times*: 'We know more about the war now, and we do not find it as amusing as we did … Whenever shows do touch on the war, they touch on it with a gravity and chastened spirit which was entirely lacking two years ago.' True, 'Keep the Home Fires Burning' was superseded as this season's most popular pantomime number by the sing-a-long hopefulness of 'Take Me Back to Dear Old Blighty', which featured in more than forty pantomime productions nationwide. Nevertheless, even when Ella Retford's Prince Fortune in *Cinderella* at the London Opera House belted out 'Tiddley iddley ighty, Hurry me home to Blighty' with 2,600 people joining in, a *Times* reporter's hunch was that 'something else lies behind the fun'. In *Puss In New Boots* at Drury Lane, the highlight wasn't Florence Smithson draped in khaki paying tribute to the new breed of working women visible on every the street in the land; it was the moment when Madge Titheradge recited the Alfred Noyes poem 'A Song of England' before a series of *tableaux vivants*:

> Whatever the artistic effect of the episode may be, the intention and quality of its patriotism are free of anything blatant, clap-trap, braggart. The inspiration is genuine, the effect is not to bounce about victory, but to extol and illustrate the labours and the sufferings demanded for victory.[5]

In fact, the theatre industry was about to labour and suffer under a series of new, often contradictory and potentially damaging demands. On the one hand, in 1917 more theatres were open than in an average peace year. [6]Just after Lauder's return to *Three Cheers!*, a *Stage* correspondent noticed that, even though the cancellation of late trains made it impossible for many suburban play-goers to visit the West End, 'It is wonderful to find how well, all things considered, the theatres are supported.'[7] On the other hand, with the authorities introducing more and more restrictive measures, most of 1917 resembled a running battle between managements attempting to keep their various enterprises on the road against increasingly difficult odds. Even so, by 1917, most rallied around the dominant narrative that by and large the stage was doing a good job at meeting the demand for entertainment while taking advantage of the new audiences created by war – that never ending stream of men on home leave, the wounded from hospitals, the convalescents from the camps and the new army of women workers toiling away in the vast new war factories who were bringing home decent enough wages to be able to spend on leisure time. Lord Derby, Minister for War, went out of his way to praise the entertainment industry as a national necessity and a tonic for returning troops: 'Let those who come home be met with cheerful faces, and let them feel that their time away from the trenches is an amusing time, that will distract them from all the anxieties and dangers they have undergone,' he told an audience of soldiers from the Dominions.[8] The common perception that war-worn civilians benefited from the relaxing powers of healthy entertainment was reinforced by a *Daily Telegraph* editorial praising the wisdom of relaxation and claiming that 'all but a significant few have earned, and need, entertainment of whatever sort best suits them'. A *Performer* editorial worried that if the theatre industry was knocked back too far by wartime restrictions, defeatist gloom would take hold: 'It would only be a matter of time, probably a few weeks, before we would become a nation steeped in pessimism, with only one thought uppermost in our minds – a too insistent longing for the normal days of peace.'[9]

Apart from constantly talking up its own therapeutic morale-boosting role, the amount of energy the industry continued to throw into fund-raising for war charities was phenomenal. By now, as *The Times* noted, theatres were the first port of call for many a good cause:

If money is needed the first idea is always a matinee at a theatre or a music hall: and time after time, the players getting nothing for their services, have raised sums of four figures in a single afternoon. The actresses, again, and such few actors as are left, are always ready to help in bazaars, sales, meetings – all the devices for raising money.[10]

By any measure, this voluntary response reached remarkable levels in 1917, with Harry Lauder's Million Pound Fund up and running and George Robey's boundless energy organising charity shows never waning, including his all-star afternoon and evening 'twin concerts': on one Sunday in March, he organised a matinee at the Palladium in aid of the Union Jack Club, followed by an evening performance at the Alhambra in aid of the Motor Transport Volunteers. By 8 August, Oswald Stoll's War Seal Foundation Fund had raised more than £42,000, enough to lay the cornerstone of the first block of homes for disabled soldiers. Ruses for squeezing cash from people became increasingly ingenious. During one week in March, the usual collections were taken at Brighton Hippodrome by uniformed nurses in aid of the local hospital: but after the Saturday night performance, leading actress Alice Delysia auctioned a tiny Pekingese dog, raising an extra £40. Shortages faced by the civilian population were not forgotten: when potatoes became scarce in 1917, veteran cockney comedienne Kate Carney not only revived one of her old coster hits 'The Baked Potato Can' on tour, but also gave away cart-loads of fresh potatoes at stage doors, all grown in her own garden.[11]

Theatres were central to the government campaign to promote the third War Loan Appeal launched in January 1917. A stirring appeal from Admiral Beatty and Field Marshal Haig was projected on the screen at all theatres on the Moss Empires circuit, accompanied by speeches from local luminaries. On Saturday, 10 February, at Shepherd's Bush Empire, nearly £7,000 was subscribed for the War Loan after one of these screenings. In the same week, one appeal took to the streets. All of the artists playing at the Finsbury Park Empire spent their Friday afternoon on a busking tour through Trafalgar Square, the Strand and

Fleet Street to promote War Loans. They stopped at various points with a barrel organ, piccolo, violin and cornet and displayed a poster with the words: 'Don't waste your time listening to us: go and put your money into the Victory War Bonds now.'

By the end of February, *The Stage* estimated that War Loans raised through theatre appeals would 'not fall far short of half a million', which included $150,000 sent by Charlie Chaplin from Hollywood.[12] When the War Savings Committee invited playwrights to do their bit, Sir Arthur Pinero came up with *Mr Livermore's Dream,* subtitled 'A Lesson in Thrift', about an wasteful overweight city type undergoing a Scrooge-like conversion after dreaming about the need for food economy. Critics derided its megaphone message, one complaining that: 'It would seem a better course to leave the theatre out of a form of propaganda that is not as convincing as it should be.' *The Times* thought Pinero's 'pamphleteering' was 'almost repulsively prosaic'.[13]

Two months later, at the St James's Theatre, Neville Chamberlain reiterated an all-to-familiar narrative strand that theatre-going was *the* panacea to wartime anxieties when he addressed a gathering of influential theatre managers and representatives from actors, variety performers, musicians and backstage organisations. The meeting had been called by Chamberlain who, as Director General of the Department of National Service, was in charge of maintaining an adequate labour force to operate vital industries. In attempting to gain support for the National Service scheme introduced in February – a form of industrial conscription that it was feared by theatre managements could lead to a 'combing out' of an already stretched workforce into designated essential industries – Chamberlain first told the audience what they wanted to hear: the stage was equal in importance to railways, mining and agriculture, adding that he considered 'amusement of the people' an essential part of national work. Even so, he went on, the industry could not carry on as normal in these abnormal times.

To some extent that part of Chamberlain's message was right. By 1917, the combination of domestic war conditions and increased government intervention in the theatrical world was turning abnormality into normality. From January, touring theatrical companies were hit by a 50 per cent increase in railway charges. New paper, printing and poster size regulations severely affected vital billposter publicity campaigns – there was even a ban on using flour as paste. By Easter, gloomy press reports implied that the government was planning to restrict performance hours in order to save electricity and coal supplies. More worrying though was the sharp increase in Entertainments Tax, introduced in order to raise an additional £1.5 million for the exchequer. All of this sounded alarm bells amid the usual panic about audiences dropping away; and the government couldn't have picked a worse time to introduce the new tax rates, when the Germans were terrifying Londoners with the first Gotha air raids. Nevertheless, as the *Daily Mirror* reported, 'Despite the agitation,

Please remember the New Order
commencing January 1st, 1917—

**NO** **CHOCOLATES** AFTER
**CIGARS OR**
**CIGARETTES** **8**

Except on SATURDAYS when
they may be sold up to 9 o'clock.

An Attendant selling them will be found
in each part of the Theatre till that time.

A programme reminder to patrons that rationing is in force. (Author)

the new Entertainment Tax came into operation yesterday. There was, however, no falling off in the audiences at those theatres which defy the Gothas and give evening performances.'[14]

When night raids began at the end of September, there was no co-ordinated action by theatres, except that everyone seemed determined to remain open, on the grounds that you were safer inside the building than outside. A few West End managements continued a matinees-only policy. Many made 'attack imminent' announcements from the stage, followed up by an 'All Clear'. Others placed printed warnings in programmes. Typically, everyone attempted to carry on despite the booms and bangs of bombs, the shriek of anti-aircraft guns and the scary sound of falling shrapnel. At the Adelphi, the audiences for *The Boy* seemed perfectly calm during a raid, according to the manager, who was particularly struck by the reaction of his women customers, who arrived laughing and chatting with their soldier friends, and 'don't seem to care at all'. At the Haymarket, the manager's only problem was preventing people watching Madge Titheradge and Lilian Braithwaite in *General Post* from rushing out to view the battle in the night sky: 'A lot of them wanted to come outside sky-gazing, and I have had the greatest difficulty in restraining them. The women are as bad as, if not worse than, the men. Really one can't help admiring their spirit.'[15] George Robey, starring in *Zig-Zag* at the Hippodrome, described the backstage atmosphere after several nights of aerial activity had turned the footlights into a firing line:

> In the midst of the hurry and scurry – girls changing methodically and behaving splendidly as though air raids did not exist; call-boy shouting 'Beginners! All down!', his voice drowned in the whizz-bang of a shell – I couldn't help thinking of the patients in hospitals, perhaps recent operation cases, and the sleepy children herded sheltering in the Tubes. Those are the thoughts that carry anger in their train, and bring the conviction that we must carry on at all costs.[16]

## AFTERNOON TEA.

A SPECIAL SERVICE OF TEA IS SERVED AT MATINÉES in all the Saloons and in the Auditorium at an inclusive charge of

### SEVENPENCE.

**To facilitate service visitors are kindly requested to ORDER IN ADVANCE.**

## AIR RAID WARNINGS.

Arrangements have been made for warning of a threatened air raid to be communicated by the Military Authorities to this Theatre.

On receipt of any such warning the audience will be informed with a view to enable persons who may wish to proceed home, or to secure better shelter, to do so.

The warning will be communicated as early as possible before any actual attack can take place. There will, therefore, be no cause for alarm or undue haste. Also to give any Naval and Military Officers whose duty requires them to go to their posts, the opportunity of immediately leaving the theatre for this purpose

Those who decide to leave are warned not to loiter about the streets, and if bombardment or gunfire commences before they reach home they should at once take cover.

The tiers and the main portion of the ceiling of the Theatre being constructed of steel and concrete, danger from falling shrapnel is remote, but those who desire more shelter than the Auditorium affords would find it in the Corridors, Bars, Staircases etc., as follows:—

In the **Upper Circle** and **Gallery**, the staircase corridors on each side, the two staircases leading to the street, and the Refreshment Bar at the back of the Upper Circle.

In the **Dress Circle**, the corridors on either side, the small stairways at the ends of these, and the two staircases leading to the main entrance. A few could be accommodated in the Ladies' Cloak-Room and the Refreshment Bar.

In the **Stalls**, the "Exit" Corridor on the right-hand side of the Stalls facing the Stage, the Corridor and the Refreshment Bar under the Stalls, and the Ladies' Cloak Room.

In the **Pit**, the Refreshment Bar, the stairway leading to it, and the corridors leading to the street

*All the positions indicated are entirely covered with steel and concrete.*

...round Stations—PICCADILLY CIRCUS, TRAFALGAR SQUARE, ... LEICESTER SQUARE and CHARING CROSS. ...cus Station is in The Haymarket, a few yards from the Theatre; ... the others are within a few minutes' walk.

&, Tucker Ltd.. Printers. 26 Long Acre. W.C.2

---

IMPORTANT

## NOTICE.

Under arrangements approved by the Commissioner of Police, the audience will be informed when an Air Raid is impending.

This will be indicated by turning up the Electrolier in the Auditorium for the space of one minute.

The "All Clear" notice will be similarly indicated immediately it comes through.

Should the warning be received during an interval an announcement will be made from the Stage.

This will give any Naval and Military Officers whose duty requires them to go to their posts, the opportunity of immediately leaving the Theatre for this purpose.

The audience are invited, at their own discretion, to remain in the Theatre if the "All Clear" has not been received before the end of the Performance.

The Management

Air raid notices posted in West End theatres. (Author)

Whizz-bangs were manageable: from the outset, however, Chamberlain's proposed National Service scheme was seen as unworkable. A policy of encouraging the withdrawal of workers between the ages of 18 and 61 from less essential trades in order to make up for the shortage of manpower in vital war industries was never going to fit easily within the context of the stage, mainly due to the uneven employment patterns peculiar to such a labour-intensive sector. Of course, from a government viewpoint it was desirable to recruit a new industrial army out of the existing non-essential labour pool: 'What is less important must give way to what is more important,' Chamberlain told theatre managements at the St James's Theatre meeting. But everyone took exception to his suggestion that casual labour engaged in scene shifting 'might be employed upon work more directly conducive to the war effort', and most regarded his idea of releasing 'some' theatre employees for National Service and keeping their jobs open for when they returned as a potential disaster when conscription had already created a serious shortage of backstage and managerial staff. In early 1917 a Theatrical Managers' Association survey found that the industry's manpower may not have been on its last legs but was only kept going by a severely depleted and decidedly elderly labour pool:

> The average age of pit musicians at a typical large theatre was 55 years. Apart from the women taken on to replace men, the theatre was staffed with old men, men discharged as unfit, wounded etc, and a few others due to be called up within the next few weeks. Of the entire male staff when war broke out, only one male staff remains. This theatre is by no means exceptional.[17]

In the end, even after much lobbying by the newly formed Joint Committee of the Entertainment Industry, actors, variety artists and musicians and backstage jobs were not included in the Restricted Occupations Order. Still, as a patriotic gesture, the staff of Hammersmith Palace reported themselves at the town hall and offered their services to assist with a borough scheme publicising National Service. The staff roll-call included twenty women, two men over 60 years of age, four under 18 and twelve discharged soldiers, five men in regimental bands and two special constables. The muddled National Service scheme collapsed within three months. Chamberlain resigned in August 1917.[18]

If Chamberlain imagined he was sticking up for the stage at the St James's Theatre meeting, it didn't seem that way to many in the audience when he said: 'Just as we are told to eat and drink in moderation, so I think in wartime our amusements should also be taken in moderation.' It was a fair point: the nation had, after all, entered a period of serious wartime thrift. But one can imagine the sound of impresarios' jaws dropping when Chamberlain then ordered them to return to 'the simpler forms of production which, after all, were good enough for us until a few years ago'. Perhaps he was only reflecting alarmist press speculation about the current state of the stage – either shows were

Manpower shortages in the entertainment profession gave women a chance to take centre stage on the Home Front: Ellison's All Lady Concert Party. (Author)

too conspicuously lavish when there was a pressing need for economy, or the business was teetering on the brink of what the *Daily Express* called a 'theatre slump' and the *Glasgow Herald*'s London correspondent thought was 'the most serious crisis that has arisen for very many years'. There was no evidence of things being quite so bad, either in London or in the provinces, especially considering wartime pressures on market mechanisms. A full-page feature by the *Sunday Pictorial* show business columnist 'First Player' was probably more in touch with the theatrical scene, headlined 'CAMPAIGN AGAINST THE THEATRES – NEW ERA OF ECONOMY' and sub-headed 'Look out for the cheapest show on earth':

> The general plan of action seems to be to call amusements a national necessity and to make them a national impossibility. But, really, this wholesale campaign of the gloom merchants seems to me to be much less of an itch for economy than an itch for complaint.

A *Stage* editorial waded in, calling the suggestion that theatres were in a state bordering on destitution 'a false and reckless one'. The reality could be seen in the constant queues of outside blockbuster West End shows such as *Three Cheers!*, *The Maid of the Mountains*, *Zig-Zag!* and the two *The Bing Boys are Here* sequels playing simultaneously in the West End: *The Bing Girls are There* at the Alhambra and *The Other Bing Boys* at the London Opera House. In April 1917, following the United States' entry into the war, *Chu Chin Chow* celebrated its 300th performance on 'America Day' with new American songs slotted in and the house packed with Americans. Even straight plays were attracting unprecedented audiences. *The Old Lady Shows Her Medals*, part of a J.M. Barrie triple-bill at the New Theatre, opened in the week that America joined the Allies, and was written to raise funds for victims of the war. 'Pure gold, perfectly wrought' was *The Times* verdict on this tear-jerking tale of a lonely old charwoman with no menfolk in the war to mourn who pretends to have a son at the Front. The highly controversial syphilis-themed *Damaged Goods* turned away curious patrons at the St Martin's Theatre because demand for tickets was so high. In the provinces, theatres were doing pretty well, too: the Theatre Royal Plymouth, for instance, reported record takings (£1,200 2s 6d) in April for the return visit of *Peg O' My Heart*.[19]

Calls for simpler forms of production weren't entirely out of place though in the fourth year of hostilities, especially with a daily national war bill touching £8 million and austerity measures and shortages adding to the general stressful undercurrent. With theatrical extravagance high on the news agenda, the issue was even raised in the House of Commons. Hansard recorded this exchange between flamboyant right-wing MP Noel Pemberton Billing and Prime Minister Bonar Law:

MR BILLING asked the Prime Minister whether he is aware that the sums that are now being expended on the production of variety entertainments and revues exceed in many instances the prewar expenditure on similar objects; and whether he will take steps to limit such expenditure of national labour and capital for the duration of the War?

MR BONAR LAW: Producers of entertainments of the nature referred to by the hon. Member are liable to the same restrictions with regard to the supply of labour and materials as other classes of the community.

MR BILLING: Does the right hon. Gentleman not think that it would be better at the present time to stop this wasteful extravagance on the production of variety entertainments and revues?

MR BONAR LAW: That deals with the general question as to what are necessaries and luxuries. There may be a great deal to be said for the hon. Member's suggestion, but I am not prepared to say that theatres should be closed.[20]

The *Stage* suggested that toning down luxurious fashion parades associated with revue might be a wise move: 'Those already in use before the need became more pressing can, of course, be permitted to remain, but prospective revue producers would do well to give the matter their careful attention.'[21] Accordingly, a new 'Economy Girls' routine was quickly inserted into *The Other Bing Boys*, with the chorus wearing gowns 'that have been so cleverly made that it is difficult to distinguish them from the more expensive and elaborate article'. Much publicity was given to their cost, at 12*s* 6*d* a piece. Shrewd West End producers cashed in on the 'war economy' craze. At the Ambassadors, Charles B. Cochran's topical revue £150 (with a plot loosely based on the recent entry of British troops into Baghdad), took its title from the show's pared-down budget, although a programme note conceded that Cochran had exceeded his original estimated production costs 'by £4 15*s*, or thereabouts.' At the Vaudeville, André Charlot staged *Cheep*, boasting a slim budget of just £300 and featuring American stage star Lee White singing 'America Answers the Call' while wearing a risqué 'Three Penny Dress' made of six halfpenny evening newspapers.[22]

A trench-inspired sketch in *Cheep* – 'With the Lads (God Bless 'Em)' – foreshadowed the arrival in the West End later in the year of a stage incarnation of one of the most popular cartoon characters of the war – 'Old Bill', the walrus-moustached old soldier created by Captain Bruce Bairnsfather and published in *The Bystander* magazine's weekly 'Fragments From France' series that continued throughout the war. Bairnsfather's mournfully satirical outlook was immortalised in his early drawing of two derelict soldiers sheltering in a shell-hole surrounded by gigantic explosions and arguing about improving their lot. The image and caption – 'If yer knows a better 'ole, go to it' – came from Bairnsfather's direct experience of the shell-hammered trenches around Messines and living alongside men doing their best to survive. 'I suddenly saw the ridiculous side of being so miserable in such bizarre surroundings. Noble, grand and necessary as the war may have been, to me it always seemed pathetically funny,' he recalled in his autobiography.[23]

In 1917, *The Better 'Ole*, or *The Romance of Old Bill*, became one of the biggest stage hits of the war years, but Bairnsfather's connections with theatre stretched back to long before Old Bill and his doleful sidekicks Bert and Alf had even entered his mind: as a youth he worked backstage at the Shakespeare Memorial Theatre at Stratford-upon-Avon, he was a self-confessed music hall addict and he even toured with his own red nose comedy act. While serving at the Front, soon after the cartoons appeared in printed format, he found himself once more 'strangely mixed up in the world of the theatre'. Screen projections of Bairnsfather's popular trench-sharpened penmanship were frequently featured on variety bills, invariably greeted with gales of laughter. Then Old Bill, Bert and Alf transferred seamlessly from cartoon form to living representations in revue sketches with recognisable 'Bairnsfatherland' settings. Bairnsfather himself had a hand in devising the scripts for these sketches, often writing them when on leave. In June 1916, *Half Past Eight* at the Comedy included a 'Fragments From France' sketch. Comedian John Humphries played Old Bill in 'The Johnson 'Ole, an Episode of Real Trench Humour' in *Flying Colours*, which opened at the Hippodrome in September 1916. In 'With the Lads (God Bless 'em)' in *Cheep*, however, Lee White could claim the distinction of being the first woman to play Old Bill. At the end of one song she threw tiny Old Bill rag dolls into the audience and, in July 1917, auctioned miniature khaki Bills 'at fancy prices' during the annual Actors' Orphanage theatrical garden party held at the Royal Hospital Gardens in Chelsea.[24]

There's no doubt that 1917 was Old Bill's finest hour onstage. While Lee White gave her impersonation at the Vaudeville Theatre, the character's greatest theatrical incarnation yet was appearing twice daily in a full-length musical play at the Oxford Theatre with the Shakespearean actor Arthur Bourchier playing Old Bill. *The Better 'Ole*, or *The Romance of Old Bill* was produced by Charles B. Cochran and co-written by Arthur Elliot and Bairnsfather, who designed the set, with music by Herman Darewski. The show opened on 4 August – the third anniversary of the declaration of war – and soon two simultaneous provincial tours were

Wishing they were back in Blighty: walrus-moustached Old Bill, Arthur Bourchier, with Tom Wootwell and Sinclair Cottee in *The Better 'Ole*, or *The Romance of Old Bill*. (Author)

Bruce Bairnsfather, the creator of *Fragments From France*. (Author)

also attracting full houses. When the West End production reached its 250th performance on 29 December, a wooden statuette of Old Bill, made at the Lord Roberts Memorial Workshops, was presented to every member of the audience. The show was still playing at the Oxford when the Armistice was declared.[25]

*The Times* observed how the 'Bairnsfather spirit' was perfectly reproduced onstage, with Bourchier's redoubtable old warrior offering 'a cheery example of what the British Army calls "swinging the lead" while forever twitching his walrus moustache and shuffling through the plot until it leads him to "the better 'ole" in the shape of a village inn'. For *Play Pictorial's* B.W. Findon, Old Bill's impact on audiences was as 'forcible as Falstaff, as quaint as Dogberry'. *The Stage* noted how comedy in the face of death caused 'the heartiest of laughter', especially among the numerous servicemen in the audience. War reporter Max Pemberton of the *Weekly Dispatch* also thought the humour was based on a distressing reality: 'Nightly you may see guardsman laughing and little milliners' assistants weeping, and hear the cheers of the men in khaki *who know* ... Mother and son, the son who fought, side by side, are holding hands. And he tells her proudly, "It was just like that out there".' This emotional hinterland was noticed by a *Daily Mirror* reviewer, who said it was 'beautifully staged and briskly acted. There is plenty of fun, too. But there is more than a little pathos – a pathos almost too poignant for these sad times. During one scene I found that I was seated between two weeping women.'[26]

Were women weeping because the show reminded them of their own personal grief? Were the milliner's assistants coping with the strain of uncertainty about a family member serving abroad? It's impossible to know. But the image of women weeping while everyone else around them was laughing at a 'Fragment from France in two explosions, seven splinters, and a gas attack' perhaps indicated a potency that distinguished that particular piece of comic entertainment from anything else in wartime theatre. Even before the curtain went up, the Oxford's interior took on an authentic war-like appearance: the foyer and sides of the auditorium were piled high with sandbags, corrugated sheeting and general trench litter, and walls were lined with 'Fragments' cartoons to remind audiences of the show's pencil and paper origins. Bairnsfather himself thought Old Bill struck a national nerve because: 'It was the focus on the minor absurdity, in the face of the titanic size and importance of the war as a whole that, as far as I can reason, made my stuff attractive to the multitude.'[27] Whereas others staged imaginary war scenarios – any 'real' mud on Vesta Tilley's Army boots was more likely to have come from Finchley than Flanders – Bairnsfather's characters not only exemplified a certain stroppy side of the British spirit – men 'caught up in the dreary annoyance of it all' as he called it – but his comedic take on their grim situations came out of direct experience. Many of the cartoons were drawn in the middle of action at the Somme and Ypres. Indeed, during his post-war tour of variety theatres (usually publicised as 'Creator of the Immortal "OLD BILL" In His Latest Laughalogue') Bairnsfather liked to tell audiences how it all started when he amused his men, usually incarcerated in mud like himself, by scribbling on odd bits of paper he could find. He recalled how one of his first cartoons in France was drawn on a cottage wall using soot from a chimney and oil from the butt trap of a rifle, while others were drawn in dug-outs and pinned up with bayonets. *The Better 'Ole* hit home onstage because it had that genuine whiff of front-line chimney soot and rifle oil or. As the editor of *The Bystander* wrote: 'It is not fun poked by a mere looker-on, it is the fun felt in the war by one who has been through it.'[28]

At the same time that Old Bill took up his post in the West End, another Army captain with theatrical interests returned home after four gruelling months on the Western Front to recover from shrapnel wounds suffered at Passchendaele. It would be another ten years before Captain Robert Cedric Sherriff's seventh play, *Journey's End*, reached the West End, by which time Old Bill had gone on to appear in several revues, a touring play (*Old Bill MP*) and two films. Today, *Journey's End* is seen as a timeless First World War classic. Because of its low comedy status, *A Better 'Ole* seems stuck in its time. But both were genuine fragments from France.

As the long arm of the war stretched into every aspect of daily life in 1917, theatrical connections between the fighting fronts and home turned into a veritable export–import industry. In January, Sir Frank Benson returned from a long tour of French Red Cross bases where, wearing khaki, he performed his one-man *Shakespeare's War Cry* featuring extracts from *Richard III* and *Henry V*. Back in Blighty, the classical actor made his variety debut at Brighton's Hippodrome, taking his Shakespearean 'turn' on a national tour, including a week at the London Palladium. In the same month, more than 300 serving officers and men arrived in London to depict trench scenes in a *Pageant of Empire* at the Coliseum. In August, when Harry Lauder was launching his Million Pound Fund in Britain, Martin Harvey was entertaining the troops in France with readings from Dickens. Across the Channel, the more serious 'straight' theatrical side of Lena Ashwell's YMCA-sponsored Concerts at the Front was in full swing. There was no stopping Ashwell's mission to provide the troops with what she called 'mental food – drama with a strong cultural flavour'. At the Le Havre YMCA hut, by the end of 1917 they were performing before an average of 18,000 men a month, with a repertory of sixteen plays ranging from Shaw to a version of the *Coventry Mystery Play*. Meanwhile, back on home turf, one of Ashwell's adventurous Firing Line concert parties reprised its danger zone entertainment at the Coliseum, with monologues and songs performed exactly as they had been close to the action. Subsequently, Firing Line concerts made flying visits to provincial theatres.[29] In August, in recognition of her achievements, Ashwell was awarded the Order of the British Empire, becoming the first woman to be admitted to this new Order and the first member of the acting profession to receive it.[30]

Apart from Ashwell's troubadours, by 1917 numerous Regimental and Divisional concert parties cheered up their comrades with less cerebral fare – so many that demand for costumes, wigs and make-up was in danger of outstripping supply. In August, the Music Hall Ladies Guild appealed for 'left off props or other articles from members of the profession' – they had sent so many parcels of costumes to France that their stock had run out.[31] Willy Clarkson, the West End costumier and inventor of the first 'All–British' greasepaint, began receiving requests for old costumes, make-up and wigs as soon as soldiers landed in France in 1914. After three years, demand had snowballed:

> This catering for scratch theatrical shows in Picardy and Salonika and the North Sea has grown to such a remarkable extent that it constitutes a special department of my business: and while I disposed of all my old stock free, I have been compelled to levy a nominal charge as a matter of sheer self-protection.[32]

A talented concert party in Salonika had no need to call Clarkson: according to founding member Percy Merriman, The Roosters were quite content to put on scratch shows with fragmentary props, passable frocks made from dyed mosquito netting and wigs made out of scraps of hair from the tails of mules. Formed in 1917 by men from the 17th London Regiment based at Summerhill Camp, Salonika, The Roosters' first performance was on 28 March 1917 in a YMCA marquee. The team soon made a name for themselves, which Merriman put down to: 'an absence of thrills but insistence on fun, fun and then some'. The first half followed the familiar pierrot format; the second half let rip with burlesque sketches, topical gags and monologues. Their potted pantomime, *Cinderella: or the Army Boot*, was still fondly remembered by veterans long after the war. With a few personnel changes, the group stayed together when the division moved to Egypt, usually seeing military action in between shows, and performed in Palestine during the Battle of Jerusalem in December 1917. After peace broke out, they were the only front-line concert party to carry on performing professionally in civilian life, making an even bigger name for themselves through BBC radio and gramophone recordings. The Roosters continued to broadcast and perform live for another thirty years.[33]

Fair but false: a remarkable female impersonation in a trench pantomime. (Illustrated London News Ltd/Mary Evans)

The network of garrison theatres included this one at Tidworth. (Author)

Professionally organised troop entertainment on the Home Front took a great leap forward in 1917 with the establishment of a circuit of garrison theatres under the control of the new Entertainments Branch of the Navy and Army Canteen Board, with Captain Basil Dean as senior officer in charge of the Entertainments Branch and Major Frank Towle in overall control of the Board. Dean joined the Cheshire Regiment in 1914, rising to the rank of captain, his new role following on naturally from his pre-military career as a theatre director at repertory companies in Manchester and Liverpool, and a brief spell as an assistant to Beerbohm Tree at His Majesty's in London. Dean had also helped to form a battalion entertainment unit and garrison theatres at Park Hall Camp, Oswestry, and at Kinmel Park near Rhyl (a hut-like theatre where a young J.B. Priestley spent much of his spare time during his military training). The NACB took over and refurbished existing garrison theatres, built new ones or converted redundant buildings. By August 1917, the Board was able to announce programmes at fifteen properly equipped theatres serviced by ten touring companies of professional actors on a standard £10-a-week contract, male actors of military age being either discharged soldiers or exempt from service. In October 1917, the 'Autumn Arrangements' card for Theatre No 4 on Circuit No. 1 listed visits by official light comedy, musical comedy, drama, melodrama and light opera companies. Performing twice nightly, each company had its own repertoire and Dean drafted in experienced West End producers to mount shows. Within months, well-known writers and composers were contributing to revues, including Ivor Novello. Performances were open to soldiers and to wives and family members.

Naturally, all of this came at a cost. Tickets were comparatively cheap and exempt from Entertainments Tax, which meant local theatre managers faced serious competition from what appeared to be a new subsidised sector flourishing on their own doorsteps allowing canny civilians to grab the opportunity to see professional garrison shows at bargain prices. On top of that, earlier in the war some producers had sunk money into leasing and running camp theatres on behalf of the military: now they faced compulsory purchase orders. Despite protests, they too had to accept the new arrangements. It wasn't all smooth running for Dean either. His own account of his experience in this new military-cum-show business world hints at the constant behind-the-scenes frustrations of a man of the theatre trying to make decisions within a red tape chain of command: 'The paths of professional and official conduct did not run in parallel; they crossed and re-crossed one another and sometimes ran in quite opposite directions,' he wrote in a memoir.[34] Surviving NACB internal correspondence offers fascinating glimpses of a backstage power struggle between Dean and his superior officer, apparently contradicting his orders. A curt 'I'm in charge' note from Major Towle, based at London HQ, dated 20 September 1917, reads:

I have a memorandum from you with regard to my visit to Salisbury and frankly I do not understand it. Do you seriously suggest that in my position I should go down to the Commands and not give orders or make what changes I consider necessary? Because if you do I can tell you here and now I shall not do it, nor is it my idea of doing business. I am the authorised mouthpiece of the Board and I shall give such orders as I consider necessary, of course, always advising Hqrs.

By the end of 1917, Dean was obviously still unhappy. In a letter requesting a clarifying statement about his position as Towle's deputy within the NACB command structure, he wrote:

I hope you will consider my claim for recognition in this form a just one. I have been feeling bitterly disappointed at the lack of it, considering my year's very hard work for the Board.[35]

In the spirit of Haig's 1917 New Year message to Ben Tillet, Dean and his team did eventually pull together: so well that the NACB Entertainments Branch became the model for official troop entertainment twenty years later, when it grew into the worldwide organisation of ENSA. Only this time, Dean was firmly in command.

# 5

## 1918

### Victory on the theatre front?

Monday, 5 August 1918. In virtually every theatre in Britain, the bank holiday ends with the opening of a brown envelope. At 9 p.m., all productions come to a halt. Artists line up onstage alongside backstage and front-of-house workers and local dignitaries. An official seal is ceremoniously broken and a letter removed. It is signed by Prime Minister Lloyd George, who has decided to mark the fourth anniversary of the declaration of war by arranging for the live onstage reading of a remembrance message to the Empire (delivered today because the national day of remembrance fell this year on Sunday, when theatres are closed). Given the advance publicity, everyone expects a pronouncement that an end of war is approaching. Instead, Lloyd George urges Britons to 'hold fast', which is arguably a tad more optimistic than Harry Lauder's gritty command in 1917 to 'keep right on'. The communiqué ends:

> I say hold fast, because our prospects of victory have never been so bright
> as they are today. But the battle is not yet won. Having set our hands to the

task we must see it through till a just and lasting settlement is achieved. In no other way can we ensure a world set from war. Hold fast!'

Cue cheering and communal singing of the National Anthem.[1]

It is no coincidence that a new Theatrical Propaganda Department had recently been established as part of the Ministry of Information. Under the direction of Ben Tillett (trade union leader and newly elected Labour MP for Salford), with James W. Tait (pantomime producer and co-composer of songs for *The Maid of the Mountains*) as second-in-command, the Department's purpose was to spur civilians on to even greater efforts. With hundreds of theatres roped in, Lloyd George's national pre-radio remembrance 'broadcast', with its hint of peace round the corner, had the potential to reach an easily get-at-able live audience of millions in one go. Synchronicity at the stroke of nine was never fully achieved, mainly because most cities, even small towns, boasted several theatres; and almost all variety houses operated the twice-nightly system. In Accrington, for instance, the Mayor, Chief Constable and a party of local worthies ceremoniously unsealed the brown envelope at the Hippodrome first house, then unceremoniously whizzed off to do the same at the Grand and two cinemas before returning to the Hippodrome for the second house at 9 p.m..[2]

As ever, show business was quick to sense the public mood and cash in on a new catchphrase. Within days, the Star Music Company invited performers and producers to buy sheet music for 'Hold Fast', the new 'Great "Cheer Up" song with a grand melody': Dorothy Ward created a furore when she featured it in *Happy Go Lucky* at Finsbury Park Empire. Coincidentally, remembrance weekend was the first anniversary of *The Better 'Ole* at the Oxford Theatre, where there was more onstage messaging when its authors, Captains Bruce Bairnsfather and Arthur Elliott, sent the cast a telegram from the Front:

The Song the World has been waiting for.

# THE PEACE BALLAD

# THERE'S A TRAMPING ON THE HIGHWAY

By Worton David & Lilian Shirley

Vocalists in Town call and hear it immediately.

Pro. Copy on receipt of Wire.

# THE LAWRENCE WRIGHT MUSIC CO.,

8, Denmark Street, Charing Cross Road, London, W.C.2.

'Phone: Regent 155.   Telegrams: "Vocable, Westcent.."

## BLACKPOOL'S SONG SENSATION
### WATCH IT FOR PANTOMIME!

# WHEN THE BOYS COME BACK

SUNG BY
**KITTY STORROW**
IN
JOHN TILLER & J. R. HUDDLESTONE'S
"SOME SHOW"
AT THE
WINTER GARDENS, BLACKPOOL.

CHORUS.
When the boys come back with their rifles and
their pack
They will find their slippers by the fire;
A loving welcome and a cosy chair,
And the dear home folk who will be waiting there.
When the fight is over and the vic-t'ry won,
Thanks to Tommy and to Jack,
There'll be no place like home,—
When the boys come marching back.

WIRE OR WRITE AT ONCE FOR PERMIT
TO
**FRANCIS & DAY**
138-140, Charing Cross Road, W.C.2.
Telephone: Regent 8508.

*This page and overleaf:* Vocalists kept up the optimistic mood onstage. (*The Era/ The Stage*)

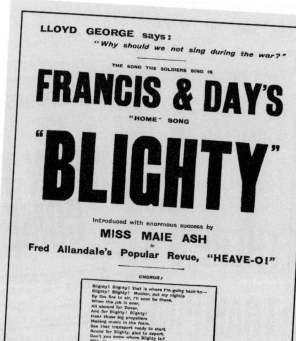

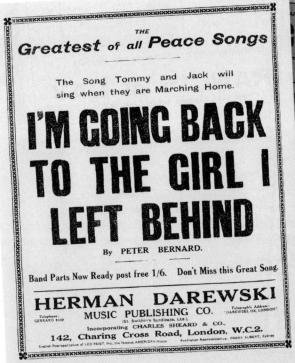

Our best wishes and congratulations to you all and the audience on this anniversary. Wish you could read the Peace Terms from the stage tonight, but meanwhile keep carrying on until we all reach a Better 'Ole.[3]

In August, when it looked as if the battlefield deadlock was beginning to break, joking about peace terms wasn't as crazy as it might seem. At home, however, the fight against a strain of Spanish influenza that had swept the country all summer looked as if it might be turning into a losing battle when it mutated into an even more lethal form; and the theatre industry wasn't immune from the deadly bug that struck without warning. West End leading lady Marie Lohr, for instance, was unable to read out Lloyd George's 'Hold Fast' message from the stage of the Globe Theatre, where she was starring in *Nurse Benson*, because she was laid low with the virus. She was lucky to have survived what was turning into a medical Armageddon: in October 1918, 2,225 people died in London alone. On Armistice Day, another wave of infection spread when large groups of people gathered to celebrate, invariably rounding off the day in the local theatre. Overall, at least 228,000 people died in Britain.[4]

On 1 July, in the same week that the entire Sunderland Empire pit orchestra was struck down with influenza, the *Daily Mirror* reported that hospitals were so overstretched that they 'could have put out the theatre sign, House Full'. Perversely, 'House Full' notices were rarely seen outside any theatre by then because people were staying away in droves from crowded places. In the absence of vaccines, all the medical authorities could do was to emphasise a need for personal hygiene and minimise the infection risk by introducing measures to curb indoor gatherings. Soon, theatres were experiencing visits from the sanitary inspector as well as policemen searching for shirkers. It took until mid July before theatres were placed out of bounds to soldiers, a restriction that had a devastating impact on attendances during the summer months of 1918. By October, the *Manchester Guardian* London correspondent wrote that 'people are fighting shy of theatres and kinemas and all kinds of meetings'. Then, as the war developed on the Western Front, leave was stopped and khaki all but disappeared from the stalls: as a *Stage* reporter noted, in Luton, 'every semblance of khaki has been completely eliminated from audiences'.[5]

No wonder. Flu symptoms could be alarming and instant, often sending infected people scurrying out of theatres midway through a performance. Few venues closed altogether. Amid growing concerns that twice-nightly shows could lead to audiences breathing a germ-laded atmosphere, by October, most local authorities issued emergency notices for places of entertainment to close between each performance. Planned matinees for the wounded had to be abandoned. Actors, many of them older because the younger ones were in uniform, suddenly succumbed to the virus. So did their understudies. Then understudies were needed for the understudies. For a time, theatres struggled, with most of their already depleted managerial and backstage staff off sick. If a variety act fell ill, a last-minute deputy turn had to be found. Sometimes so many artists were 'off' that an entire week's programme might be subject to last-minute changes, as a bemused critic from *The Era* discovered during a tour of south London music halls at the height of the flu scare:

> Whenever 'Deputy Turn' is announced I get a little thrill of pleasurable excitement. The possibilities are so endless. For you may see anything from Little Titch to the worst woman in London, from Lockhart's Elephants to the great new star you've dreamt for years of discovering.

Some stage folk found flu's funny side. As the mounting death toll began to appear in the papers alongside the daily lists of losses on various war fronts, *The Era* joked that its 'song of the moment' was 'Everybody's 'Fluing It'; and when monologist Bransby Williams starred at Liverpool Hippodrome in July (his eldest son, a captain in the Royal Flying Corps, was killed in 1917), items that he auctioned in aid of the Mayor's Prisoners of War Fund included a box inscribed 'Bransby Williams' Cure for the Flu'. It turned out to contain a flue-brush.[6]

At this juncture, flu was no laughing matter for managements when commercial survival meant contending with a new barrage of restrictions and economy measures, all introduced to reflect the ever-changing priorities of the war economy; but none designed to make life any easier for producers, actors and performers already feeling the strain on numerous fronts. Things looked very gloomy indeed when a new Lighting, Heating and Power Order proposed 'lights out' in theatres at 9.30 p.m., with a requirement that lighting usage should be one-sixth less than in the previous year. This curfew was soon changed to between 10.30 p.m. and 1 p.m. the following day. Even so, it still meant either an early 'curtain up' or shortened shows, partly because of people having to get home when late public transport was severely reduced in towns and cities where blackout plans were strictly enforced. London's theatre district was shrouded in more gloom at night than ever before. On his first trip to the West End, an American journalist was struck by how 'a few carefully hooded lights indicated the theatres, which formerly presented blazing facades'. It took a test case at Chichester County Police Court for the authorities to concede that a flicker of after-show lighting could be allowed backstage when removing scenery used by touring companies: the police had caught the proprietor of Bognor's Kursaal Theatre using six illuminated electric bulbs at 11.15 p.m. when 'striking' a touring company's sets. Even so, according to the odd logic of an *Era* editorial, braving dark streets and going out to a theatre was a way of keeping cheerful and far more patriotic than sitting at home and shivering in the dark to save lighting and heating costs:

> Our theatres and music halls are, in point of fact, communal sitting rooms in being. At the Lyceum Theatre, for example, some three-thousand citizens congregate each evening in a single chamber. By so congregating, they are performing an involuntary and unconscious act of patriotism, for they are saving the vast waste of coal and electricity and gas which would eventuate if each unit remained in his own particular home.[7]

Next, an unbelievably complex set of new restrictions on the use of paper threatened to hit crucial theatre advertising. These measures were modified when the Controller of Paper allowed theatre programmes to be printed at a reduced size on medium-quality paper and posters could be produced on the back of old stock, provided they bore the imprint: 'Printed on the reverse side of posters which were in stock before March 2, 1917.' Then another wartime measure – the Sale of Sweetmeats in Theatres (Restriction) Order, 1918 – threatened an already uneven source of additional income from the sale of confectionary, cigars and cigarettes after 8 p.m..

Much harder to swallow was food rationing, which brought unforeseen consequences for touring theatricals criss-crossing the country every week. In April 1918, a full ration book registration scheme came into effect, adding meat, butter, cheese and margarine to an already growing list, with special arrangements for food served in boarding houses. Food coupons were eventually issued for people travelling from place to place, but performers in touring companies often found themselves at the end of the queue, only to see local tradesmen giving preference to their own clientele, which led one touring manager to complain: 'Naturally what food they have they allow their own customers first: the artists get nothing. Some of my people tell me they have had no meat for three weeks.' Fred Karno made fun of it all in a new touring revue starring Robb Wilton called *Rations*, later changed to *Coupons*, with one spicy sketch depicting the rationing of kissing.[8] Even where food was available on ration, the clutch of wartime measures could transform eating out before or after a West End show from a popular ritual into a frustrating non-event, as American journalist Milton Valentine Snyder explained when he wrote to his wife in Paris in February 1918:

As all London theatres begin at such early hours that it is almost impossible to dress, dine and be there on time, I went without my dinner and was frightfully hungry when the show was over. I went across to the Trocadero, anticipating a good supper. Alas! such things no longer exist. I could get

One printing firm came up with a solution for theatre companies facing paper restrictions. (*The Era*)

no meat, nothing hot is served after 9.30 o'clock and when I ordered a
Russian salad was told that it could not be served as it contained meat. I
had some eggs and a piece of cheese.[9]

Inevitably, the cost of lodgings skyrocketed. Never among the well-
paid in the industry, touring actors often arrived in a town to find that
rooms were at a premium, partly due to the influx of war workers and
military billeting schemes, but mainly thanks to profiteering landladies
who, according to theatre impresario Arthur Gibbons: 'charge exorbitant
prices for very meagre accommodation, very often without lighting
or attendance'. War or no war, you either paid up or: 'as some chorus
ladies I know of were told not long ago "You can walk the streets"'.
Landladies were the target of one angry letter to *The Stage*, signed 'One
Of Many', complaining of arduous train journeys followed by long hours
searching for 'digs', then having to appear onstage and sleep overnight in
a dressing room: 'I know of a few landladies, who owe their success to the
professionals who are now turned down in favour of the cowards of air
raid refugees and other newcomers.'[10]

At least by now performers and audiences had grown accustomed to
German bombing raids accompanied by flying shrapnel and the roar
of 'Archies' (anti-aircraft guns) pounding away. In London's West End,
the Criterion Theatre advertised itself as a safe haven 'built entirely
underground' and became home to regular matinees for wounded
soldiers. The 'Cri' was not, therefore, among the theatres that abandoned
evening performances on Saturday, 16 February, when air-raid warnings
sounded and a Zeppelin-Staaken 'Giant' aircraft flew across the West End
to drop a bomb on the Royal Chelsea Hospital. When the alarm was first
raised there were cheers and cries of 'carry on' at one West End theatre:
hardly anyone took advantage of the management's invitation to remain
in the building until the 'All Clear' signal was given. Some theatres
allowed patrons to take shelter until well after midnight.[11] At a time
when some 300,000 Londoners were routinely using the Underground
system for overnight shelter, this attack caught Milton Valentine Snyder

in a theatre where, shortly before the final curtain, it was announced that a raid was imminent:

> Few persons left immediately. When we did come out the streets were, if anything, darker than usual; crowds of people were hurrying towards the Tube stations and in front of the theatre two 'bobbies' repeated monotonously: 'Take cover.' I went to Leicester Square Tube station to see how the foreign dwellers in Soho were taking the warning. They had the scare good and hard and were jamming and crushing into the entrances, blocking the exits and filling every passageway: a heaving, apprehensive-eyed mass of smelly men, women and children. [12]

Next month, on the moonlit night of 7 March, searchlights picked out another German 'Giant' flying high above an unlit West End. The aircraft moved on and dropped two bombs further afield, both scoring a direct hit on a terrace in Warrington Crescent, Maida Vale. Homes were completely destroyed, thirty-three people were injured and twelve were killed instantly, including the poet Lena Guilbert Ford, who wrote the lyrics to 'Keep the Home Fires Burning', and her disabled 30-year-old son. Here was the saddest of ironies: the song that had bankrolled Ivor Novello received a new lease of life in 1918 when America entered the war, yet the American-born woman who dreamed up the words made hardly a penny because she never established her right to royalties. On the fatal night of the bombing, there was no 'silver lining, through the dark clouds shining' for Ford, who returned home early after attending a West End matinee. She had been working on a new song, 'We Are Coming, Mother England', to welcome her fellow Americans into the war, which she hoped would be taken up theatrically and make her financially secure. She also wrote lyrics for 'Tommy's Mail Day' (promoted as the 'Great post-bag song') with violinist Phyllis Nash. By another twist of fate, Nash was performing the song in one of Lena Ashwell's Firing Line troupes on the night that Ford was killed. [13]

Meanwhile, Novello combined his new desk job at the Air Ministry with occasional visits to France as one of Ashwell's players. But composing was his real war work. In his spare time Novello wrote music for (and appeared in) patriotic fund-raising pageants, including *The Pageant of Freedom* at Queen's Hall during 'Women's Week for the Wounded' in 1918, and *The Treasures of Britain* at the Shaftesbury Theatre, in which he played Lancelot. By then, at the age of 25, Novello had become an in-demand West End songsmith, contributing melodious numbers for the revues and musicals that made West End theatre a magnet for escapist entertainment seekers. After supplying a new song for *The Bing Boys are Here*, he established himself as a promising composer with *Arlette*, an operetta in three acts with 'plenty of agreeable melody',[14] and the long-running wartime hit *Theodore & Co*, co-composed with an equally youthful Jerome Kern. During 1918, the West End revue, sometimes called 'revuette' or 'revusical', reached its zenith. Hugely attractive to war-weary soldiers on leave, especially the shows produced by André Charlot and Charles B. Cochran, they offered light, fast-moving topical sketches, songs, comic turns, dance sequences and lots of gorgeous chorus girls. *Tabs*, which opened at the Vaudeville in May 1918, was mostly performed in front of austerity-inspired black drapes, with Novello's songs providing the 'general brightness and irresponsible spirit' and topical sketches such as a send-up of the lighting curfew, a burlesque of a German spy play, an American soldier song ('Sammy'), and Beatrice Lillie mimicking an RAF officer. In 1918, Novello also contributed songs for *Tails Up!*, a bubbly entertainment at the Comedy Theatre starring Jack Buchanan, Teddie Gerrard and Phyllis Monkman, notable because it included the first publicly performed song composed by Noël Coward, 'Peter Pan'. Both shows were still running in November when the Armistice was announced.

Not everyone appreciated the novelty and allure of wartime revue, seen by some as lewd and suggestive and likely to lead soldiers into immoral ways. In early 1918, E.A. Baughan of the *Daily News* expressed a loathing for the formulaic silliness of the genre: 'If only revue writers could manage to connect their numbers by a central idea the revue would be more entertaining than it is. The inconsequence of most of these pieces is a little trying.'[15] Thomas Burke would have nodded in agreement. Writing in his *London Notebook*, he described Novello-type wartime revues as nothing more than mediocre laughter machines driven along by lazy performers:

> They dazzle the eye and blast the ear, and, instead of entertaining, exhaust. The artists have, allowing for human nature, done their best under trying circumstances; but playing to an audience of overseas khaki and tired working-people, who applaud their most maladroit japes, has had the effect of wearing them down. They take the easiest way, knowing that any remark about the Kaiser, Old Bill, meat-cards, or *The Better 'Ole* is sure of a laugh.[16]

But then Burke, an avid pre-war theatre-goer and prolific recorder of everyday London life, derided wartime productions in general:

> At one time I loved a show, however cheap its kind; but in these days, after visiting a wartime show and suffering the feeling of assisting at some forbidden rite, I always wish I had wasted the evening in some other manner. Since 1914 the theatres have not produced one show that any sober man would pay twopence to see.'[17]

He was probably thinking of the spy plays, which were still running into the 1920s. Typical was the long-running *Inside the Lines*, by American novelist Earl Derr Biggers (the creator of Charlie Chan detective novels), which was set in Gibraltar and involved spies attempting to blow up the entire British Grand Fleet on its way to the Black Sea. But *By Pigeon Post*, about German spies in a French château pretending to be French soldiers and using secret cyphers, camouflaged carrier pigeon cupboards and hidden wireless equipment, was praised by the *Daily Telegraph* for being 'one of the most ingenious that the present struggle has produced'.[18]

There seemed to be a conveyor belt of German spy plays. (Author)

It's not true that only spy dramas, fluffy musicals and saucy revues succeeded during the war years. According to *The Tatler*, many theatre-goers were fed up with standard fare, jingoism and Hun-phobia. They were still prepared to go and see something 'real' in the theatre, 'something with foundations laid deep down in the human heart of things'.[19] Had Burke popped along to the Oxford Theatre in the West End at the end of June 1918, he would have come across a surprisingly deep playlet dropped into the second act of *The Better 'Ole. The Kiddies in the Ruins*, a dramatic playlet depicting the plight of orphaned children in the war-ravaged villages of France, was identified by critic E.A. Baughan as one of several dramas in which the war genuinely became part of the 'web and woof' and not merely an 'applied decoration'. Adapted by Brigadier-General J.E. Cannot from a French play (a film version was released later in the year, just after the Armistice) it does at least suggest that some dramatists weren't shying away from dealing with social and psychological issues. Even so, you'd be hard pressed to find anything onstage dealing with current domestic politics: 1918 was, after all, the General Election year, when some women were allowed to vote for the first time. In January, playwright Gregory Piessipoff did explore a Russian revolutionary theme in *Annajanska, The Bolshevik Empress* at the Coliseum, with Lilla McCarthy starring as an empress who throws in her lot with the Reds. 'Piessipoff' turned out to be Bernard Shaw, who also directed.[20]

Some playwrights looked ahead to an imagined post-war Britain where demobbed servicemen would return to their homes almost as strangers. Herbert Thomas's *Out of Hell*, opening at the Ambassadors in January 1918, explored the anxiety of mothers discovering that their soldier sons might never again be what they were when they left for the Front – a domestic situation picked up comedically in A.A. Milne's *The Boy Comes Home* at the Victoria Palace, in which an angry young ex-warrior goes into battle with the older generation. Given that death had touched an entire nation, it also stalked the stage. J.M. Barrie's haunting one-act séance drama *A Well-Remembered Voice* tapped into the surge of interest in spiritualism and the often unspoken experience of people carrying on with life surrounded by the memories and ghosts of lost loved ones. In *Roxana,* at the Lyric, a young woman's husband who she told everybody was dead, turns out to be alive in Florida. Even the musical comedy *Soldier Boy!*, at the Apollo, featured an officer who pretends to be dead. Other serious dramas touched on marital fidelity, gender insecurities and the changing role of women in society. In *Reported Missing* by John F. Preston and Florence Davis, a British officer escapes capture and returns home to find a nightmare situation where his wife is about to marry another man. Similarly, Mrs F.G. Kimberley's *A Soldier's Divorce*, which opened on Armistice night at the Elephant and Castle Theatre, emphasised the patriotic need for marriage after the fighting was over. The sense of a possible change in the established male order of things was far more cleverly handled in Harold Brighouse's *Hobson's Choice*,

Even the flu epidemic couldn't curtail the end-of-war euphoria. (*The Stage*)

which examined the growing domestic and economic empowerment of a new generation of women; although Henry Esmond's 1918 romantic comedy *The Law Divine*, at Wyndham's Theatre, warned wives to return to the pre-war gender status quo (prophetically as it turned out), by not becoming so engrossed in work that they neglected their husbands in peacetime. Similarly, in *When Our Lads Come Marching Home*, by the Irish dramatist Sheila Walsh, it is staid home-girl Peggy who ends up in a happy post-war marriage rather than her twin sister Elsie, whose good-time lifestyle during the war leads to misery.[21]

By all accounts, when peace did finally break out on 11 November, there was quiet disbelief on the battlefronts. Towns and cities across Britain, however, exploded as soon as maroons went up at 11 a.m. and people streamed out of workplaces, taking to the streets to celebrate. Catching on faster than Spanish flu, by evening the end-of-war euphoria had spread everywhere. This was not, though, a holiday for theatre workers: local theatres became rallying points for a communal release of pent-up emotions. In Manchester, offices, shops, mills and munitions factories closed and the city was rocked by scenes of jubilation. By evening, playhouses and variety theatres were heaving with Mancunians, none of them giving the flu warnings a moment's thought. Few paid much attention to what was actually happening onstage at the Theatre Royal (*The Luck of the Navy*, a spy play), the Gaiety (*Damaged Goods*, the shocking drama about syphilis), The New Queens (a musical version of Ethel M. Dell's *The Way of an Eagle*), the Palace (*Be Careful Baby!,* a farce), or the Hippodrome (top billing, Bransby Williams in a *Seven Ages of Man* sketch). A *Manchester Evening News* reporter doing the rounds found: 'The packed and hilarious audiences often got out of hand, and made their own entertainments with hysterical singing and patriotic songs, frantic cheering and flag waving and impromptu speech-making.'[22]

In Portsmouth, the King's Theatre audience of men in khaki and naval blue roared and cheered at every anti-Kaiser gag in Fred Karno's *Kill or Cure*, while *The Hustlers* concert party based at Clarence Pier had to give up when a crowd of servicemen took over the stage and performed their own impromptu concert. As ever, theatre producers and sheet music publishers were quick off the mark. A new fifth act, entitled *Peace With Victory*, was instantly added to a touring production of *Under Orders* by Herbert Thomas. Star Music released 'Jubilation Day' by A.J. Mills and Bennett Scott almost as quickly as Lawrence Wright Music rushed out Worton David and Lilian Shirley's 'Song that will lead them home' entitled 'There's a Tramp, Tramp, Tramp Upon the Highway'.[23]

In London, where *Chu Chin Chow* was in the eleventh week of its third year at His Majesty's and *The Maid of the Mountains* (still advertising itself as an 'all British production') was nearing its third year at Daly's, *The Stage* noted a 'peculiar rapport between audience and the stage … every theatre could have been filled twice over'. Matinees and early first houses were cancelled. Instead, long queues of singing, cheering people formed outside for the evening performances. Later, with lighting restrictions lifted, theatre porticoes blazed for the first time in years, windows were lit up once more and searchlights ranged overhead. Roving reporters from *The Times* called in at theatres and found interiors decked in flags and pent-up audiences 'a-quiver with half-suppressed feeling, and ready to give it vent as fully as they could'. It only needed one person to interrupt the show and kick-off with 'Land of Hope and Glory' and the entire audience was on its feet and joining in. Any mention of peace onstage resulted in huge cheers.[24] The audience watching *The Better 'Ole* at the Oxford 'yelled itself hoarse' when Old Bill himself read out a special letter from the author:

> Best wishes to you all and to the audience. A far, far better 'ole has been found at last. – Bruce Bairnsfather.

During intervals, theatres with projection facilities showed pictures of the Allied leaders followed by images of the Kaiser – head downwards. At the Palladium, comedian Billy Merson quickly inserted a song about the Kaiser into his pirate routine. Ella Shields' act at the Holborn Empire slotted in a new number, 'The Shade of Nelson', with the stirring line:

'England's still the mistress of the sea'.[25] At the Coliseum, 3,000 people stood for the appearance onstage of the 2nd Division Canadian Concert Party and Orchestra giving excerpts from their revue, *We Should Worry*; the troupe arrived direct from the fighting lines to share top billing with Diaghilev's Ballets Russes. At Drury Lane the audience was reluctant to go home after a performance of the spectacular operetta *Shanghai*, only agreeing to leave after an appeal from the manager. There were raucous scenes at the Middlesex music hall until the manager, an ex-serviceman himself, called for a tribute to those who had died for the cause. Soldiers removed their caps, civilian men held their hats and the entire audience stood in silence for one minute.[26]

A 'House Full' sign stood outside the Alhambra for *The Bing Boys on Broadway*, but inside a restive, festive audience was continually on the hop between the seats and the bars. George Robey, the show's star, recalled an atmosphere as carnivalesque as in the streets outside:

> Nobody on the stage could take his or her work seriously. We all "ragged" and "gagged" in a way that defied Art and Discipline, and even the playing of the orchestra seemed to be, as they say, all over the shop … altogether the evening was one of the strangest in all my experience.

Later on, making his way home through a West End still full of revellers, Robey felt as strangely distant as he did on the night war was declared, his head full of people he would never see again: 'I felt more like crying than singing and dancing. Nor could I help thinking of the millions of people who, at that moment, behind windows closed and curtained, were thinking of their dead.'[27]

But it was over. Job done. Actors, performers, writers, musicians, stage workers at every level and from all backgrounds, men and women, had entertained the nation at home and abroad. Many laid down their lives. Some won medals for bravery. Others returned from battlefields and prison camps severely maimed, mentally scarred or broken in health, unable to follow their profession ever again. Theatre had overdosed on

## TILL THE BOYS COME HOME (2).

Keep the home-fires burning, while your hearts are yearning,
Though your lads are far away they dream of home;
There's a silver lining through the dark cloud shining:
Turn the dark cloud inside out, till the boys come home.

BAMFORTH COPYRIGHT.                    BY KIND PERMISSION OF ASCHERBERG, HOPWOOD & CREW, LTD.

patriotism, while raising millions for war funds. The industry helped keep the public, the forces and the hospitalised in good spirits, while working within unprecedented manpower limitations, makeshift conditions and financial restrictions. When peace finally arrived, *The Stage* believed that theatre had been a barometer of the state of the war.

> When the news was bad the theatres were empty; when the news was good they filled again; and at the end of 1918 a stall was more difficult to buy than a box of matches. We were lifted on a wave of theatrical prosperity.

Three days after the Armistice, the King acknowledged the achievements when he made a point of taking a royal party to see George Robey in *The Bing Boys on Broadway* and told Sir Oswald Stoll, who was knighted in 1919: 'I felt anxious to show my personal appreciation of the handsome way in which a popular entertainment industry has helped in the war with great sums of money, untiring service, and many sad sacrifices.'[28] Yet peace was not the final curtain: it was the start of a new beginning. Post-war demobilisation and reconstruction not only meant remembering the valiant dead who once trod the boards; it meant rebuilding a theatre industry by and for the valiant living.

# Epilogue

# When the Boys (and the Girls) Came Home

Monday 17 February 1919. The foyer at the Theatre Royal Drury Lane resembles a chapel of rest. Flowers are everywhere. Mourners include vicars of local churches, actors and theatre workers. The hush will evaporate soon when the matinee audience charges in to see *Babes in the Wood* ('The Great Peace Pantomime'); but right now the Bishop of London, Arthur Foley Winnington-Ingram (a fervent jingoistic supporter of the war), is quietly unveiling an imposing mahogany wall-mounted Roll of Honour dedicated to the actors, musicians, stage hands and clerical staff who have fallen. The heroic lines on the centre panel end:

> They nobly played their parts; These heard the call
> For God and King and Home they gave their all.

Either side are inscribed the names of men who worked in theatres all over London: there are 253, although more will be added over time to bring the total to 302. After paying tribute to the theatrical profession's war record, the Bishop concludes by saying that he would tell any widow or mother whose boys never came home: 'Let the note of triumph conquer the note of sorrow.' Then singer Harry Dearth leads the congregation in 'Land of Hope and Glory', followed by four buglers sounding the Last Post.[1]

Three months after the Armistice, when the remains of the dead were being interred in war graves in France, the triumphalism of peace had turned to a long drawn-out national service of remembrance. In his study of the war's social impact, *British Culture and the First World War*, George Robb argues that a highly elaborated ritual of honouring the fallen developed in the years following a conflict that was 'more aggressively memorialised and commemorated that any war before or since'. Memorials grew up spontaneously everywhere; some connected to a theatre industry in mourning, although the ceremony at Drury Lane provoked mixed feelings in a representative from *The Stage*. He complained about a lack of support from leading actors, who were conspicuous by their absence on 'an occasion which was a solemn and dignified moment in the history of the stage in connection with the great war'.[2]

As time went by, the Drury Lane Roll of Honour became an annual focus for remembrance. In 2014, when the centenary of the declaration of war was marked by a special Armistice Day service, another generation of theatre workers mingled in the same foyer alongside the relatives of two of the men listed on the memorial, including small part actor Walter George Woodgate, who was killed on his twenty-first birthday in 1918 whilst delivering messages along the front line as a private in the Cyclist Corps; his name is given equal billing alongside Guy du Maurier, author of the *An Englishman's Home* in 1909, William Dartnell, the first actor to be awarded a VC, and actor–playwright Harold Chapin. This time, after a brief address, there was no Last Post, no National Anthem; just a quiet rendition of Ivor Novello's soundtrack to the war years, 'Keep the Home Fires Burning'.[3]

In 1931, the Drury Lane stage itself became a site of collective remembrance when a First World War sequence in Noël Coward's *Cavalcade* featured 'Keep the Home Fires Burning'. During the 1930s a conveyor belt of lavish Novello musicals kept the theatre busy, ending with *The Dancing Years*, which ran for so long that it became the *Chu Chin Chow* of the Second World War. Great War memories re-emerged yet again when the theatre reopened in 1939 as the base for the Entertainments National Service Association (ENSA), sending out organised entertainment for serving personnel and war workers, with Basil Dean (by then the country's leading theatre director) in command, reprising his First World War Garrison Theatres scheme on a global scale.

Over time, one of the few physical memorials dedicated to actors was lost and presumed missing. The Green Room Club for theatricals commissioned eminent sculptor and memorial designer Ferdinand Victor Blunstone to create a plaque in honour of twelve club members who died in various theatres of war, including Lionel Mackinder, whose name also appears on the Drury Lane Roll of Honour and was one of the first actors to die in action when he was hit by a sniper in January 1915. After moves to several different premises, this impressive art nouveau bronze memorial became separated from the club, whereabouts unknown; but in 2010 it suddenly turned up as 'Lot 722' in a sale of ephemera at an auction room in Rugby, where an unknown buyer paid just under £1,000 for it.[4]

The first Salvation Army-organised battlefield pilgrimage to visit the graves of relatives on the Western Front left London in April 1920, in the same week that the first West End play to tap into the collective memory of the war opened at the St Martin's Theatre. Directed by Basil Dean, *The Skin Game* by John Galsworthy, portrayed a gloves-off, no-winners conflict between social classes in which the victors are as crushed as the vanquished, and was seen at the time as an allegory of the war. *The Times* critic was left feeling 'as if you've been living in a war neighbourhood where the people begin to throw stones without waiting to see if they live in a glasshouse'.[5] *The Skin Game* was still playing to full houses on 11 November 1920 when the most significant national outpouring of remembrance took place after the unveiling of the Cenotaph in Whitehall. As part of the commemoration, the remains

The plaque erected in memory of members of the Green Room Club ended up decades later as Lot 722 in auction. (John Frearson)

of the Unknown Warrior were interred at Westminster Abbey with great ceremony, at the end of which the grave was covered by an embroidered white silk funeral pall presented to the Abbey by the Actors' Church Union and inscribed: 'Given in memory of actors who fell in the First World War.' Afterwards, almost the last visitors to pay their respects were a party of disabled residents from the Oswald Stoll's War Seal Mansions in Fulham, which by then was so overwhelmed with disabled ex-services applicants that Stoll abandoned plans to construct a theatre nearby and instead used the land to add a further sixty-four flats.[6] *The Stage* was in no doubt that the building was a 'lasting monument' to a profession that played a vital role in raising the cash to build it.[7] A century later, the Stoll charity still provides housing for services veterans and has expanded beyond recognition. The only clue to the charity's wartime theatrical origins is a large memorial plaque on the exterior façade dedicated to some of those who contributed to the scheme's success, including Vesta Tilley and Forget-Me-Not Day collections organised by the Music Hall Ladies Guild.

The memory of theatre's wartime charitable role was not so easily forgotten. The 1919 Royal Variety Performance at the Coliseum specifically celebrated 'the generous manner in which the artists of the variety stage have helped the numerous funds connected with the war'.[8] One artist not invited to perform or take part in the concluding 'Pageant of Peace' spectacle was Marie Lloyd, who had been snubbed at an official post-war dinner held in honour of theatre professionals who had raised money or entertained the troops. After George Robey spoke at length, she stood up and complained about receiving no recognition for her own considerable war efforts, which included numerous Sunday charity matinees and shows for munitions workers: 'Apparently, in this war neither poor old Ellen Terry nor poor old Marie Lloyd have done anything – except the gentleman who has just spoken to you. This is not strictly correct.'[9] 'Our Marie' walked out. The profession's charitable habit didn't end there. In January 1920 an annual 'Warriors' Day' scheme was launched at Drury Lane to support Field Marshal Haig's British

Oswald Stoll's War Seal Mansions opened in 1917. Queen Mary visited an early intake of wounded ex-servicemen in 1919. (Stoll)

Legion Fund. Thought up by Sir Herbert Beerbohm Tree's widow, the idea was for every theatre in the country to give a matinee in aid of the Fund. Thousands of special performances were held over a several days at the end of March and Lady Tree eventually handed Hague a cheque for £115,140 on the stage of His Majesty's Theatre. As an annual appeal, Warriors' Day was soon superseded by Haig's Poppy Day. [10]

Performers continued donating their time as morale-raisers well into the 1920s, only more often than not they faced rows of severely wounded ex-servicemen, many suffering from terrible facial and bodily disfigurements. After the war, Lady Tree organised weekly concerts at the vast King George military hospital in south London, where George Robey found that his comic songs could undo the effects of shell shock.

Robey also entertained patients at Queen Mary's Hospital in Sidcup. Here surgeons were pioneering plastic surgery techniques on men who were so disfigured that they rarely went out in public. On one memorable occasion, Robey invited a party of patients to the Hippodrome where he was starring in the post-war celebratory revue *Joy-Bells* (hit song, 'Goodbye, Khaki'). The former soldiers and sailors were hidden from public gaze behind a curtain so they could see the show but not be seen.

The Stoll Foundation today: a lasting monument to a profession that played a vital role in raising the cash to build it. (Author)

During the performance, Robey spent his off-stage time with the group, which included one man who had endured numerous operations having his face rebuilt: 'Fortunately his eyes had been spared, and afterwards, when I got to know them quite well, I gave him the nickname of "Merry-Eyes", which his comrades in the hospital took up. They said it helped him.' Many artists carried on raising cash to support victims of war; Robey continued his wartime gala charity shows at the Coliseum. In November 1920, a note in the programme for a matinee in aid of the children of print workers who had been killed explained that the performance aimed to show that 'although memories are short, and the hours crowded with new incident, there are some debts that we cannot and never will forget'.[11]

Without the daily emergency of war, with the spirit of victory dying down, and faced with national reconstruction, the post-war theatre industry went into peacetime recovery mode. On the ground, homecoming actors and performers returning to an industry run by mostly elderly staff and women often found themselves in terrible straits trying to find employment, leading to a slew of 'Situations Wanted' advertisements in the theatrical press. It didn't help when Ministry of Reconstruction demobilisation procedures downgraded actors and theatre staff deemed not to be involved in essential work for speeding up the economic recovery. Many actors began to think they had nothing to show for their sacrifices: some spent the rest of their acting lives with body parts missing or with recurring symptoms from injuries. While flying bombing missions over German lines, actor–aviator Robert Loraine received gunshot wounds to a knee that left him out of action for almost a year until he returned to the West End in March 1919 to play the dashing lead in *Cyrano de Bergerac* – with one kneecap missing. Casting the play was difficult because suitably fit actors for the principal parts were still away at different fronts.[12] Some war-disabled British actors eventually became stage and film stars. Ronald Colman was hit by shrapnel in his foot: he attempted to hide his limp for the rest of his Hollywood career. Claude Rains never fully recovered from a gas attack that left him partially blinded. Herbert Marshall was a battlefield amputee, but returned to the London stage four months after the Armistice with a prosthetic leg. Playwright and actor Arnold Ridley resumed his acting career after suffering a bayonet attack at the Somme that left him without the use of three fingers: in his later years, he played Private Charles Godfrey in the BBC sitcom *Dad's Army*.

At the top end of the theatre industry, the transition to peacetime saw the beginnings of a decline in the dominant pre-war actor–manager model and the ascendancy of the powerful theatre syndicates. According to a *Sunday Express* survey of the West End, there were thirteen actor–managers in the season of 1913–14; by 1919 there were only six.[13] With the industry's corporate players now calling the shots, there was probably some truth in theatre critic Huntly Carter's assessment that, in terms of ownership, post-war British theatre had become 'largely a soulless machine joined to the Stock Exchange'.[14] At the end of 1919, soaring land values and inflated rents led to a post-war boom in theatre real estate deals. Theatres constantly changed hands: 'five West End theatres are either for sale or have been sold,' reported the *Express* in October 1919; by January 1920, the *Daily News* reckoned the boom 'appears to be at its height'. As a result, to remain profitable, theatres began to lose their distinct pre-war identities: old music halls were turned into straight playhouses; variety theatres presented revues; playhouses staged musicals. The lavish long-running show with star names that emerged during the war as a recipe for filling theatres began to dominate, just when live entertainment was being hit hard by cinema and, from 1922, radio. This shift towards even greater commercialism, however, also saw the beginnings of a move towards a different form of independent non-commercial, often experimental, theatre that eventually grew in strength to redefine and reshape the entire British theatre environment.

The war years more or less called to a halt the activities of small independent club theatre companies and dramatic societies that had presented new plays, the work of foreign dramatists and classics, usually for a limited number of performances and often on Sundays. Pre-war aspirations for a National Theatre were suspended. But a new kind of theatre emerged that was rooted in the trenches and grew out of the activity around organised troop entertainments. When you knew that productions could be mounted in crowded camp huts or tents filled with smoke and packed to suffocation; when former professionals had got used to devising theatricals of all kinds in improvised conditions on the tiniest of budgets; and when soldier audiences grew to accept that you didn't need to be in a neo-classical auditorium to buy into a dramatic performance, it's not surprising that some of this experience transferred to post-war theatre.

The repertory movement began to flourish and independent play-producing organisations such as the Stage Society found a new lease of life. Under the auspices of the British Drama League, formed in 1919, numerous non-commercial Little Theatres and smaller repertory companies appeared in unlikely places, offering an alternative experience to the commercial West End and provincial touring theatres. The League aimed to 'assist Development of the art of the Theatre and to promote a relation between Drama and the life of the community' and was formed after its founder, Geoffrey Whitworth, attended a wartime play reading given by munitions workers and saw that acting and theatre didn't have to be the pastime of a leisured few but could become the recreation of many.[16] A good example of this approach in action was the Everyman Theatre in Hampstead, founded in 1920 in a former drill hall, where the works of Eugene O'Neill and Luigi Pirandello were introduced to British audiences and Noël Coward had his first success, *The Vortex*, in 1924. It was no accident that these independent theatres and play-producing societies were in the forefront of presenting serious new work that both memorialised and asked questions about the war. The Everyman premiered the stage version of Captain Richard Berkeley's *The White Chateau*, set in the destroyed Fourth British Army headquarters at Hooge, a drama that carries the distinction of being the first radio play. Before the broadcast by the London 2LO radio station on Armistice Day 1925, *The Radio Times* noted that:

The White Chateau will be remembered by all ex-Service listeners who remember Hooge. This Radio Drama promises to provide a powerful interpretation of the transition from war to peace.[17]

The Repertory Players produced two important 'lost generation' plays: Harry Wall and A.L. Muir's *Havoc* in November 1923, before it transferred to the Haymarket Theatre; and Hubert Griffith's *Tunnel Trench* (1925) at the Prince's Theatre, which was revived as the opening play for the new Duchess Theatre in 1929, when R.C. Sherriff's *Journey's End* was also playing in the West End following its original staging by the Stage Society.

As one of the first elected vice-presidents of the British Drama League, Lena Ashwell carried over her Concerts at the Front war experience to peacetime. By creating theatre outside of the mainstream, she pioneered the idea of professional companies supported by local authorities as a civic amenity, rather like libraries. When the arts were expected to support themselves commercially, this was a revolutionary proposal for a municipal theatre, or 'recreation for the people' as Ashwell described her Once-a-Week Players (later known as the Lena Ashwell Players). Between 1920 and 1929, three separate fit-up companies performed classics and contemporary plays at affordable prices in town halls and boarded-over public swimming baths in the poorer London boroughs and as far afield as Jersey and Wales. At the start, all of her actors were ex-soldiers: their attitudes to theatre and acting, she believed, had changed as a result of their experience of the squalor of battle. These men weren't hankering after stardom, they wanted to be 'of service to people rather than be run after by them'. The key women running the operation had all been involved with Ashwell's Concerts at the Front and the company ethos harked back to the shoestring simplicity of those productions, with everyone working as a team and 'the stage setting consisting of curtains, with just a few articles of furniture indispensable for the proper presentation of the play'.[18]

This was never, of course, a profitable enterprise. There was always a shortfall between running costs and box office income, which had to be made up by donations, charitable grants and Ashwell's own Reconstruction Fund. Local authority rates were not supposed to be used to subsidise municipal drama either, but Ashwell argued that's exactly what they should be doing: she also talked idealistically about 'People's Theatres' that would be 'as plentiful as libraries'. Prophetically, she envisaged a theatre that was socially and educationally 'useful to the community' that would 'leave the commercial theatre untouched financially, but give them a larger and more appreciative public'.[19]

The project failed financially; but Ashwell's was an inspired and inspiring voice in the between-the-wars debate about establishing non-commercial local repertory theatres and a National Theatre that she believed 'should be the final apex of a system of civic co-operation in every borough, town, and city'.[20] It took many more decades for a link between state subsidy and the arts to become a natural part of Britain's theatrical landscape. Ashwell made the historic first practical steps towards forging it; and they can be traced straight back to British theatre at war and to the lived experiences that emerged from the holocaust of 1914–18.

# Notes

## Prologue

1. *Daily Mirror*, 28/29 January 1909.
2. *The Stage*, 30 January 1909.
3. *An Englishman's Home: a play in three acts*, Major Guy du Maurier (Harper) 1909.
4. *Daily Express*, 29 January 1909.
5. *The Times*, 28 January 1909.
6. *The Observer*, 31 January 1909.
7. *Daily Express*, 30 January 1909.
8. *New York Times*, 21 February 1909.
9. Hobson, J.A. *The Psychology of Jingoism* (Grant Richards) 1901, p4.
10. *The Times*, 28 January 1909. *Illustrated London News*, 6 February 1909.
11. *Daily Express*, 6 February 1909.
12. Williams, Rohdri, *Defending the Empire*, Ebury Press (1998), p125.
13. *The Play Pictorial*, February 1909.
14. Mead, Gary *The Good Soldier*, Atlantic Books (2008), p152.

15. *Daily Express*, 8 February 1909.

16. Ibid.

17. *Daily Mirror*, 29 January 1909.

18. Ibid, 12 February 1909.

19. *Daily Express*, 10 February 1909.

20. *An Englishman's Home*, programme material (1909), Westminster City Archive, London.

21. *Daily Express*, 20 February 1919.

22. *Manchester Guardian*, 23 February 1909.

23. *The Observer*, 21 February 1909. *The Stage*, 25 February 1909.

24. *The Times*, 24 February 1909.

25. *Daily Mirror*, 28 February 1909.

26. *The Stage*, 18 February 1909.

27. *Daily Mirror*, 29 February 1909.

28. *Daily Express*, 29 February 1909.

29. *The Stage*, 8 March 1909.

30. Ibid, 12 March 1915.

31. *Oh! What a Lovely War* programme (1963).

# 1. 1914

1. MacDonald, J. Ramsay, *The Man of Tomorrow*, Leonard Parson (1923), p100.

2. Robey, George, *Looking Back on Life*, Constable (1933), p146.

3. *The Era*, 12 August 1914. *The Stage*, 27 January 1916.

4. *Manchester Evening News*, 5 August 1915.

5. French, David, *British Economic and Strategic Planning 1905–1915*, Allen & Unwin (1982).

6. Davis, Tracy C., *Edwardian Management and the Structures of Industrial Capitalism*, in *The Edwardian Theatre: Essays on Performance and the Stage*, eds: Michael R. Booth and Joel H. Kaplan, Cambridge University Press (1996), p111–129.

7. Roberts, Robert, *The Classic Slum: Salford Life in the First Quarter of the Century*, University of Manchester Press (1971), p148.

8. *The Era*, 19 August 1914. *The Times*, 5 August 1914.

9. *The Stage*, 20 August 1914.

10. Ibid, 3 September 1914.

11. Ibid, 20 August 1914.

12. Ibid, 3 September 1914.

13. Loraine, Winifred, *Robert Loraine: Soldier, Actor, Airman*, Collins (1938), p177.

14. *The Stage*, 13 August 1914.

15. Ibid, 27 August 1914.

16. Ibid, 28 September 1914. Walton, John K., *Blackpool*, Carnegie Publishing Ltd (1998), p110–111.

17. *The Era*, 16 September 1914.

18. *The Stage*, 8 October 1914.

19. *The Era*, 30 September 1914.

20. *The Stage*, 20 August 1914.

21. *West End and Friedrichstrasse: A comparative study of popular theatre in London and Berlin, 1890–1939*. Cross-cultural Exchange in Popular Musical Theatre, 1890–1939 Conference, 2012. www.gold.ac.uk/research/popular-musical-theatre/conference

22. *The Era*, 19 August 1914.

23. Robey, George, p151.

24. *The Era*, 9 September 1914.

25. Ibid, 16 September 1918.

26. Ibid.

27. Ibid, 12 August 1914.

28. *The Era*, 2 September 1914.

29. *The Stage*, 13 August 1914.

30. Ibid, 20 August 1914.

31. *The Era*, 16 September 1914.

32. Ibid, 19 August 1914.

33. Ibid, 12 August 1914. *The Stage*, 13 August 1914.

34. *The Stage*, 27 August 1914.

35. *The Era*, 9 September 1914. *The Stage*, 17 December 1914.

36. Ibid, 16 September 1914.

37. Begbie, Harold, *Fighting Lines and Various Reinforcements*, Constable (1914), p13.

38. *The Stage*, 13 August 1914. *The Era*, 12 August 1914.

39. Noble, Peter, *Ivor Novello: Man of the Theatre*, Falcon (1951), p53–71. *Daily Mail*, 1 December 1915.

40. *The Observer*, 20 December 1914.

41. *The Stage*, 24 December 1914.

42. *The Times*, 28 December 1914.

## 2. 1915

1. *Daily Mirror*, 6 January 1915.

2. *Richmond Time-Dispatch*, 7 February 1915.

3. *The Stage*, 7 January 1915.

4. Ibid.

5. Ibid, 15 May 1915.

6. Robinson, Paul, *Military Honour and the Conduct of War: From Ancient Greece to Iraq*, Routledge (2009), p159.

7. Chapin, Harold, *Soldier and Dramatist: Being the Letters of Harold Chapin*, John Lane (1917), p61.

8. *Leach's Lady's Companion*, December 1915. Terriss, Ellaline, *Just a Little Bit of String*, Hutchinson (1955), p215–225.

9. *The Stage*, 7 January 1915.

10. Ashwell, Lena, *Modern Troubadours: A Record of the Concerts at the Front*, Gyldendal (1922), p33.

11. Ibid, p7.

12. Ibid, p36.

13. Ibid, p10.

14. Ibid, p10–11.
15. *Daily Sketch*, 20 September 1915.
16. Ashwell, Lena, p114.
17. Goodliffe, J.B., *The Voice*, 8 September 1918.
18. Ibid.
19. Cited in Fuller, J.G., *Troop Morale and Popular Culture in the British and Dominion Armies 1914–1919*, Clarendon Press (1990), p21–31.
20. Flanagan, Bud, *My Crazy Life: The Autobiography of Bud Flanagan*, Frederick Muller (1961), p71.
21. *The Stage*, 22 April 1915.
22. Ibid, 3 June 1915.
23. *The Era*, 30 June 1915.
24. Legge, Edward, *King Edward, the Kaiser and the War*, Grant Richards (1917), p108.
25. *The Stage*, 7 October 1915.
26. Ibid, 12 September 1915.
27. Henson, Leslie, *Your Faithfully*, Long (1948), p56. Rose, Clarkson, *With a Twinkle in My Eye*, Museum Press (1951), p66.
28. Haymarket Theatre programme 1915, Westminster City Archive, London.
29. *Punch*, 15 September 1915.
30. *The Era*, 2 June 1915.
31. Arthur, Max, *Forgotten Voices of the Great War: Told by Those Who Were There*, Random House (2012), p91.
32. Lauder, Harry, *A Minstrel in France*, Andrew Melrose (1918), p42–45. *The Era*, 10 July 1915.
33. Palace Theatre programme, Manchester City Library Archive. de Frece, Lady Matilda (Vesta Tilley), *Recollections of Vesta Tilley*, Hutchinson (1934), p137–145.
34. *Manchester Guardian*, 20 November 1917.
35. Hook, John, *The Air Raids on London During the 1914–1918 War*, Booklet No 5: *The Raids on the City of Westminster*, City of

Westminster Archives (1987). Henson, Leslie, *Yours Faithfully,* John Long Limited (1947), p53.

36. *The Bystander,* 5 January 1916.
37. *The Times,* 12 September 1915.
38. Graves, Robert, *Goodbye to All That,* Jonathan Cape (1929), p110.
39. *The Times,* 2 January 1916.
40. *Daily Express,* 27 December 1915.

# 3. 1916

1. *Daily Express,* 3 January 1916.
2. *Daily Express,* 3 January 1916. *The Times,* 4 January 1916.
3. *The Stage,* 20 January 1916. *The Times,* 18 January 1916. *The Era,* 3 February 1916.
4. *The Era,* 16 April 1916. *The Stage,* 18 April 1916.
5. *Everywoman's Weekly,* 14 April 1916.
6. 'The English Bernhardt', *Black and White,* February 1894.
7. *The Stage,* 20 April 1916.
8. *The Era,* 1 March 1916.
9. Playne, Caroline E., *Society at War 1914–1918,* Allen and Unwin (1931), p107.
10. *The Era,* 31 May 1916.
11. *The Era,* 5 January 1916.
12. *The Era,* 28 June 1916.
13. *The Era,* 24 May 1916.
14. *The Stage,* 3 March 1916.
15. *The Era,* 12 April 1916. *The Play Pictorial,* No 166, Vol XXVII (1916).
16. *The Stage,* 18 May 1916.
17. Shaw, George Bernard, preface to *Heartbreak House: A Fantasia in the Russian Manner on English Themes,* (1919), Floating Press edition (2009), p19.

18. *The Play Pictorial*, No 166, Vol XXVII, January 1916.

19. *The Stage*, 25 May 1916.

20. *The Play Pictorial*, No 172, Vol XXIX, No 166, May 1916, p3.

21. *The Stage*, 7 June 1917.

22. Barker, Felix, The House that Stoll Built, Frederick Muller (1954), p126.

23. Bate, Jonathan, *The Genius of Shakespeare*, Pan Macmillan (2008), p197.

24. *The Sphere*, 22 April 1916.

25. Hendley, Matthew, *Cultural mobilisation and British responses to cultural transfer in total war: the Shakespeare tercentenary of 1916*, International Society for First World War Studies, 3 January 2012, pp25–49. www.firstworldwarstudies.org.

26. *The Era*, 3 May 1916, p11.

27. *The Era*, 2 February 1916. *The Stage*, 11 May 1916.

28. *Daily Express*, 27 May 1916.

29. *The Stage Yearbook*, 1917.

30. Barker, Felix, p125.

31. MacDonagh, Michael, *In London During the Great War: The Diary of a Journalist*, Eyre and Spottiswoode (1935), p123.

32. *The Stage Yearbook* (1917).

33. *The Era Annual* (1917).

34. Robey, George *Looking Back on Life*, Constable (1933), p171.

35. MacDonagh, Michael, *In London during the Great War*, Eyre and Spottiswood (1935), p171.

36. *The Observer*, 3 September 1916.

37. *Chu Chin Chow* programme (1916), City of Westminster Archives, London.

38. Lauder, Sir Harry, *A Minstrel in France*, Andrew Melrose (1918), p70–75.

## 4. 1917

1. *The Times*, 4 January 1917.
2. Lauder, Harry, *A Minstrel in France*, Melrose (1918), p80–89. *The Times*, 4 January 1917.
3. Lauder, Harry, p109–118. *Aberdeen Evening Express*, 9 July 1917.
4. Lauder, Harry, p134–144.
5. *The Times*, 4 January 1917.
6. *The Stage Yearbook* (1918).
7. *The Stage*, 11 January 1917.
8. Ibid, 1 February 1917.
9. Ibid, 1 February 1917.
10. *The Times*, 29 November 1916.
11. *The Stage*, 22 March 1917.
12. Ibid, 22 February 1917.
13. Ibid, 18 January 1917. *The Times*, 16 January 1917.
14. *Daily Mirror*, 2 October 1917.
15. *The Stage*, 27 September 1917.
16. *Daily Mirror*, 3 October 1917.
17. *The Stage*, 29 March 1917. Grieves, Keith, *The Politics of Manpower 1914–18*.
18. *The Stage*, 22 March 1917.
19. *Glasgow Herald*, 9 April 1917. *Sunday Pictorial*, 8 April 1917. *The Stage*, 19 April 1917. *The Stage*, 9 April 1917. *The Stage*, 12 April 1917.
20. *The Observer*, 4 March 1917. *Hansard*, HC Debate, 1 March 1917, vol 90 cc2142–3.
21. *The Stage*, 29 March 1917.
22. Ibid, 26 April 1917. Tanitch, Robert, *London Stage in the 20th Century*, Hans Publishing (2007), p53.
23. Bairnsfather, Bruce, *Wide Canvas*, John Lane (1939), p64.
24. Ibid, p68.
25. *The Stage*, 29 November 1917.

26. *The Times* 6 August 1917. *The Play Pictorial*, September 1917. *The Stage*, 20 September 1917. *Daily Mirror*, 6 August 1917.
27. Bairnsfather, Bruce, p67.
28. *The Times*, 30 January 1917. *The Bystander's Fragments From France*, Vol 1, 1917.
29. *The Stage*, 18 October 1917. *The Times*, 13 December 1917.
30. *The Times*, 4 December 1917.
31. *The Stage*, 30 August 1917.
32. *The Era Annual*, 1918, p95.
33. *The Great War … I was There!*, Volume 3, Sir J. Hammerton (ed), Amalgamated Press (1939).
34. Dean, Basil, *The Theatre at War*, George G. Harrap (1956), p18.
35. The Basil Dean Archive, John Rylands University Library, University of Manchester.

# 5. 1918

1. *Manchester Guardian*, 6 August 1918.
2. *The Stage*, 8 August 1918.
3. Ibid.
4. Honigsbaum, Mark, *A History of the Great Influenza Pandemics: Death, Panic and Hysteria, 1830–1920*, I.B. Tauris (2013), p187–210.
5. *Sunderland Daily Echo and Shipping Gazette*, 2 July 1918. *Daily Mirror*, 1 July 1918. *Manchester Guardian,* 30 October 1918. *The Stage*, 28 October 1918.
6. *The Era*, 10 July 1918.
7. Ibid, 11 September 1918.
8. *The Stage*, 7 February 1918.
9. Snyder, Alice Ziska and Snyder, Milton Valentine, *Paris Days and London Nights,* E.P. Dutton & Co (1921), p56.
10. *The Era*, 18 September 1918. *The Stage*, 8 August 1918.
11. Snyder, Alice Ziska and Snyder, Milton Valentine, p56.

12. Ibid, p58.

13. *New York Times*, 13 March 1918.

14. *The Times*, 7 September 1918.

15. *Daily News*, 18 January 1918.

16. Burke, Thomas, *Out and About; a note-book of London in war-time*, George Allen & Unwin (1919), p67–68.

17. Ibid, p67.

18. *Daily Telegraph, 2* April 1918.

19. *The Tatler,* 21 August 1918.

20. *The Stage*, 14 November 1918. Barker, Felix, *The House That Stoll Built*, F. Muller (1957), p130.

21. *The Stage*, 14 November 1918. *The Times*, 18 October 1917.

22. *Manchester Evening News*, 11 November 1918.

23. *The Stage*, 14 November 1918.

24. *The Times*, 12 November 1918.

25. *The Era*, 13 November 1918.

26. *The Stage*, 14 November 1918. *The Times*, 12 November 1918.

27. Robey, George *Looking Back on Life*, Constable (1933), p179–180.

28. *The Stage Yearbook* (1919).

## Epilogue

1. *The Stage*, 20 February 1919. *The Times*, 18 February 1919. *Yorkshire Evening Post*, 17 February 1919.

2. Robb, George, *British Culture and the First World War*, Palgrave (2002), p208–217. *The Stage*, 20 February 1919.

3. Information kindly supplied by Mark Fox, Really Useful Theatres.

4. Frearson, John P.H., *The Green Room Plaque: A Memorial to Twelve Actors of the First World War* (2014), John Frearson Publishing.

5. *The Times*, 22 April 1920.

6. *Western Daily Press*, 19 November 1920. *Nottingham Evening Post,*

27 March 1920.

7. *The Stage*, 8 August 1918.

8. *The Stage*, 17 July 1919.

9. Jacob, Naomi, *'Our Marie' (Marie Lloyd)*, Hutchinson (1937), p213.

10. *The Stage*, 24 March 1921.

11. Robey, George, *Looking Back on Life*, Constable (1933), p181–189.

12. Loraine, Winifred, *Robert Loraine: Actor, Soldier Airman*, Collins (1938), p250.

13. *Sunday Express*, 5 January 1919.

14. Carter, Huntly, *The New Spirit in the European Theatre*, Ernest Benn (1925), p68.

15. *Daily Express*, 30 October 1919. *Daily News*, 24 January 1920.

16. Martin Browne, E., *The British Drama League, Educational Theatre Journal*, Vol. 5, No. 3 (1953), p203–206.

17. *The Radio Times*, 9 October 1925.

18. *The Era*, 11 August 1920.

19. Cited in Leask, Margaret, *Lena Ashwell: Actress, Patriot, Pioneer,* The Society for Theatre Research (2012), p167–205.

20. Ashwell, Lena, *The Stage*, Geoffrey Bles (1929), p176.

# Select Bibliography

Adie, Kate, *Fighting on the Home Front: The Legacy of Women in World War One* (London: Hodder & Stoughton, 2013).

Arthur, Max, *Forgotten Voices of the Great War* (London: Ebury Press, 2002).

Ashwell, Lena, *Modern Troubadours: A Record of Concerts at the Front* (London: Gyldendal, 1922).

Baker, Richard Anthony, *Marie Lloyd: Queen of the Music Halls* (London: Hale, 1990).

Barker, Felix, *The House That Stoll Built* (London: Frederick Muller, 1954).

Carter, Huntly, *The New Spirit in the European Theatre 1914–1924* (London: Ernest Benn, 1925).

Chapin, Harold, *Soldier and Dramatist: Being the Letters of Harold Chapin* (London: John Lane, 1917).

Cooksley, Peter, *The Home Front: Civilian Life in World War One* (London: The History Press, 2013).

Dean, Basil, *Theatre at War* (London: George Harrap, 1956).

Dean, Basil, *Mind's Eye: An Autobiography, 1927–1972* (London: Hutchinson, 1973).

De Frece, Lady Matilda (Vesta Tilley), *Recollections of Vesta Tilley* (London: Hutchinson, 1934).

Double, Oliver, *Britain Had Talent: A History of Variety Theatre* (London: Palgrave, 2012).

Ervine, St John, *The Theatre in My Time* (London: Rich & Cowan, 1933).

Flanagan, Bud, *My Crazy Life* (London: F. Muller, 1961).

Frearson, John P.H., *The Green Room Plaque* (John Frearson Publications, 2014).

Fuller J.G., *Troop Morale and Popular Culture in the British and Dominion Armies, 1914–1918* (London: Clarendon, 1990).

Henson, Leslie, *Yours Faithfully* (London: John Long Limited, 1948).

Hudd, Roy, *Music Hall* (London: Eyre Methuen, 1976).

Jones, Nigel, *Peace and War – Britain in 1914* (London: Head of Zeus, 2014).

Lauder, Harry, *A Minstrel in France* (London: Melrose, 1918).

Leaske, Margaret, *Lena Ashwell: Actress, Patriot, Pioneer* (London: Society for Theatre Research, 2012).

Legge, Edward, *King Edward, The Kaiser and the War* (London: Grant Richards, 1926).

MacDonagh, Michael, *In London During the Great War: The Diary Of A Journalist* (London: Eyre, 1935).

Macqueen-Pope, Walter James, *Carriages at Eleven: The Story of the Edwardian Theatre* (London: Hutchinson, 1947).

Major, John, *My Old Man: A Personal Journey into Music Hall* (London: William Collins, 2012).

Martin-Harvey, Sir John, *The Autobiography of Sir John Martin-Harvey* (London: Sampson Low, Marston and Company, 1933).

Mead, Gary, *The Good Soldier: The Biography of Douglas Haig* (London: Atlantic Books, 2007).

Miller, Ruby, *Champagne From My Slipper* (London: Jenkins, 1962).

Millward, Jessie, *Myself and Others* (London: Hutchinson, 1923).

Playne, Caroline E., *Society at War 1914–1918* (London: George Allen & Unwin, 1931).

Poel, William, *What Is Wrong With the British Stage* (London: George Allen & Unwin, 1920).

Priestley, J.B., *The Edwardians* (London: William Heinemann, 1970).

Robey, George, *Looking Back on Life* (London: Constable, 1933).

Rose, Clarkson, *With a Twinkle in My Eye* (London: Museum Press, 1951).

Short, Ernest Henry, *Ring Up the Curtain: Being a Pageant of English Entertainment Covering Half a Century* (London: Jenkins, 1938).

Stone, Christopher, *Christopher Stone Speaking: Autobiographical Reminiscences* (London: E. Matthews & Marot, 1933).

Tanitch, Robert, *London Stage in the 20th Century* (London: Haus Publishing, 2007).

Terriss, Ellaline, *Just a Little Bit of String* (London: Hutchinson, 1955).

Winter, Jay Murray, *The Great War and the British People*, (London: Palgrave, 2001).

Wyke, Terry and Rudyard, Nigel, *Manchester Theatres*, Bibliography of North West England (Manchester ,1994).

# About the Author

**Roger Foss** is a former actor turned theatre journalist. As an actor he worked in rep, summer seasons, the West End and television. He also wrote and appeared in pantomimes at Watford, Colchester, Chesterfield and Croydon, all before obtaining an MA in Modern Drama at Essex University. He has written and broadcast on theatre and entertainment subjects for numerous publications ranging from *What's On In London* magazine and *The Stage*, to whatsonstage.com, LBC and BBC Radio London. He was chief theatre critic for whatsonintheatre.com, editor of *What's On Stage* magazine and is the author of *May the Farce Be With You* (Oberon Books) and, with Mark Shenton, *Hardens Theatregoers' Handbook* (Hardens).

#tilltheboyscomehome
@fossroger

# Index

If you enjoyed this book, you may also be interested in…

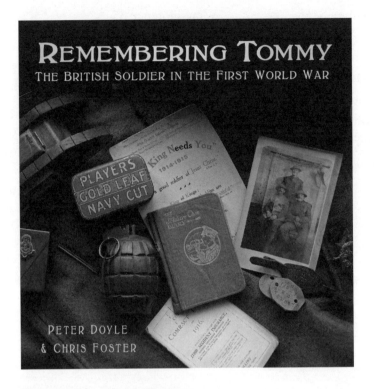

## Remembering Tommy

PETER DOYLE & CHRIS FOSTER

978 0 7509 8146 0

The British soldier of the Great War has been depicted in many books. Invariably, a pen picture paints him as stoic, joining the army in a wave of patriotic fervour, and destined to serve four years on the Western Front. Yet often the picture is difficult to resolve for the reader. How did the soldier live, where did he sleep? What was it like to go over the top, and when he did, what did he carry with him? For many, the idea of trench life is hazy, and usually involves 'drowning in mud'. *Remembering Tommy* pays tribute to the real British soldier of the Great War. In stunning images of uniforms, equipment and ephemera, it conjures the atmosphere of the trenches through the belongings of the soldiers themselves – allowing us almost to reach out and touch history.

The destination for history
www.thehistorypress.co.uk